Holy Living

Simplicity

Wendy J. Miller

Elaine A. Heath
General Editor

HOLY LIVING: SIMPLICITY

ISBN 9781501877667

Manufactured in the United States of America

19 20 21 22 23 24 25 26 27 28—10 9 8 7 6 5 4 3 2 1

ABINGDON PRESS
Nashville

TABLE OF CONTENTS

FOREWORD

From the time that individuals began responding to Jesus' call to follow him, they began to learn rhythms of life that would be essential for them to be able to live their lives wholeheartedly for God. Chief among these practices was prayer. Jesus modeled for them how to withdraw from busy service to spend time alone in prayer. He offered prayer verbally in front of them, and when they asked, taught them to pray with the prayer we now call the Lord's Prayer. Following Jesus' ascension, as the disciples waited in Jerusalem "for what the Father had promised," that is, the Holy Spirit, Luke tells us that "all were united in their devotion to prayer" (Acts 1:4, 14). Prayer was foundational and formational, positioning them to receive the Holy Spirit, God's empowering presence that both indwelled and propelled them.

Following that transformative event, in due time they followed the Spirit's leading and bore witness to Jesus "to the end of the earth" (Acts 1:8). Their lives were busy, on the move, teaching, preaching, healing, explaining, encouraging, and confronting the evil and injustice of their society. Yet all of that doing, they knew, had to emanate from a deeply grounded experience of being. Nurturing a loving relationship with God was a central commitment that they, like we, had to learn to practice. Apart from this relationship, their busyness was meaningless. So they and those who followed them in the faith added to the practice of prayer a wide range of spiritual disciplines to strengthen their relationship with God, help them grow in Christlikeness, and fuel them for the work God called them to do.

Some of these practices—things like meditation, simplicity, and fasting—are more inwardly focused. Others are expressed outwardly and corporately—things like confession and worship. And some of the practices can be both, such as prayer. All of them—and there are many—work together to help us achieve lives of balance, anchored securely to Christ and equipped for meaningful engagement with others.

This book is one in a series, each volume focusing on a single discipline. In this volume, Wendy Miller invites us to step into the path of simplicity, wherever we are, and evaluate our relationship with things, ourselves, others, God, and indeed all of creation. I invite you to join this journey and learn to listen to the voices that inform these relationships.

—Elaine A. Heath

INTRODUCTION
Holy Living: Simplicity

All journeys begin somewhere, and the pathway to simplicity begins where we are now rather than where we wish we could be. This pathway may begin with an awareness of fatigue, along with a nagging frustration about having too much and too little space, overcrowded closets, and a crowded storage unit we haven't touched for five years. Or, it may be the problem of never having enough no matter how many hours we put in at a low-paying job. On the other hand, we may be moving houses due to a job change or even because we are retiring and moving from the "family house" to a retirement center. We realize as we pack that we have way too much stuff—hence, the need to decide on what to keep, what goes in the yard sale or to the thrift store, what gets given away, and, finally, what goes in the trash.

Some of us find ourselves working three jobs with a family to raise. The days only have so many hours, the week only so many days. How do we discover joy and satisfaction in the midst of so much work, so much to do, so little time?

Any of these challenges can begin to look like a problem we wish would just go away. But rather than ignoring the problem, we do well to honor what this "voice" is saying. If we pause to listen to what the problem is telling us, we notice that its fist begins to open up, and we discover the voice of longing waiting in its palm to greet us. The voice of longing is kind, does not condemn or judge, but invites us to consider a pathway that could offer some guidance for a way forward. Our desire for simplicity is being awakened. We are crossing the threshold onto a pathway that leads toward simplicity.

The pathway to simplicity is not a straight and linear road. It may well be that, at first, this path draws our attention into the world of the kitchen, the garage, the front closet, or the outside work shed—into the actual doing of the work where we desire change. The outward path calls on us to become aware of our relationship with things. The world around us encourages our accumulation of things and at the same time offers us advice on how to downsize, to become simple, uncluttered. The world's voices are mixed and inconsistent. Hence, we will be paying attention to the clutter of the voices of the world around us as we travel together.

The pathway to simplicity also leads us into our inner world as we make decisions about how to start this work, and then more decisions as we are in the midst of sorting; or as we make decisions to figure out how to find help as we struggle with working at a low-paying job and not being able to keep up with the bills.

> It's complicated because there is too much to do, too many tasks . . . I can't keep up with it all . . . I feel burdened, sometimes even guilty...And I think maybe I'm doing it wrong.[1]

Hence, on this journey we will encounter other voices within the inner world of the heart, the soul. We will discover that this inner pathway awakens us to our relationship with our self, with others, with God, and finally, with creation. Simplicity is the gift which emerges within the larger sphere of relationship.

As we begin, know that we are on a pilgrimage, walking the outward and the inward pathways together. Embedded in each chapter are spaces which invite personal reflection. We are not reading primarily to get the job done, but also for inner discovery. The pauses for reflection offer guidance for you for that inner path, which in turn helps clarify the path for the outward journey. At the close of each chapter, I invite you to have a conversation with your community. Bring to the conversation your reflection and prayer, sharing with one another what you are discovering as you walk the outward and inward paths.

CHAPTER ONE
Beginnings

Pay attention to how you listen.
(Luke 8:18a)

VOICES OF THE WORLD WE LIVE IN

In today's world, our desire for change can lead us to the find ads about clearing out clutter. (That is what our overload of possessions is now named.) This is actually a popular trend, and we can even find help with this venture. A move toward "simple" can be a step in that direction. Here, we will also encounter other voices. When the number of these ads promising simplicity reaches a critical mass, then simple becomes a trend, an "in" thing.

Behind the scenes and the voices of the world—magazines, books, and multiple computer websites which offer advice about pruning (clearing out clutter)—another voice is at work; a second litany is being sung. Simple is in. If you want to be in, simple is the path. Sign up for our advice. Now another longing is being lured into consciousness: we want community—to be in somewhere—with others. This is the desire of the inner self: the inner world.

A Japanese consultant, Marie Kondo, has done much work in this area, and her approach has attracted the attention of persons in this country.[1] Her advice has struck a needy chord in our yearning for something simpler, better, easier. KonMari is now a brand: a voice which promises life-changing magic that will tidy up your house and bring you joy. This trend and how-to advice can be delivered to one's in-box for anyone who desires to sign up. Kondo also offers advice on how to maintain the new, uncluttered space.[2]

Many persons have picked up on this idea—so much so that this voice is also shaping how real estate agents guide their clients. When we were preparing to sell our house of nineteen years in a rural area of Virginia, the real estate agent reminded us that we would need to stage our house. Being on stage brought up images in my mind of being involved in a drama and acting out a script—in front of an audience. There is some truth to that. Following that script translated into renting a storage facility in which to pack various pieces of furniture from our large, sunny living room, except for one love seat and one armchair. Other rooms also needed to be staged—furniture items from bedrooms, the dining room, even pictures on the walls—all were now to be out of the house and stored. The built-in cabinets and bookshelves in the living room were to be emptied, save for one bowl or two books on each shelf. We were told that people—the audience who would be looking at our house—are not able to imagine their furniture, pictures, and so forth in a house containing another person's items.

If we are working many hours and also raising a family, what other help might be available? We don't have an overload of possessions or an overload of anything, for that matter. So, how does simplicity fit within our ever-present reality? We find ourselves needy on so many levels. What voices bombard our lives? Where can we find counsel?

Jim was manager in a bank, was married, and had two sons—one in junior high and the other in high school. His wife, Lisa, enjoyed a part-time job working in the grade school. They also enjoyed a rich social life in the suburbs of a major city. Their income was adequate and even allowed for family vacation in the summers. But then, Jim was laid off. The bank was downsizing, and Jim found himself unemployed. And the line at the job-search center was long. Pretty soon, their savings were running low, they could no longer afford the mortgage payment, and a sudden high medical bill caused their financial pantry to be bare. They moved out of their house and tried to find an inexpensive place to rent, but Lisa found that she could not face the stress, the loss of the house, the suburbs, the times with her friends, and she finally left the marriage. Jim was left alone to cope. He found himself falling under the line of having enough, a place in life he had never imagined.

He applied for unemployment, subsidized housing, and spent much of his time filling out job applications.

In the meantime, he found that feeding three men—two of whom were teenagers and growing fast—was more than he could afford. But going to a food bank? That was out of the question. But was it? Finally, he found out where the closest food bank was and decided to go. To Jim's surprise, the space inside was large and well-stocked and open on that day. When the man behind the counter asked if he needed help, Jim said he was just looking. He found it too hard to admit his need. The voice inside his head said, *Men are supposed to be able to cope.* However, Bob at the front counter, quietly aware of the fear of newcomers to the food bank, left the counter after a while and walked over to where Jim stood staring at a shelf of breakfast cereals. Bob waited at a slight distance, and then in a quiet voice said, "I see you've found the breakfast shelf." Then gesturing to the shelf across the aisle, Bob said, "Over on this side, you'll find the breads, muffins, and so on. And to make things convenient, here's the peanut butter and jellies on the next lot of shelves." Jim turned to Bob, beginning to feel appreciation for this kind and respectful voice as Jim tried to find his way in this never-before-visited place in the world.

"I hate to admit this, but this is just the aisle I need. I have two sons who wolfed down the last of the cereal this morning." Jim could hardly believe what he had just said. Now what would this guy think of him?

"I get it," said Bob. "I'm glad for the job here after losing my job because of downsizing due to business relocation. This food bank is one of the best in town—arranged more like a store, and you are free to find and choose what you need. We're open Saturdays and Wednesdays. I'm Bob, and I work here part-time."

Jim swallowed the lump in his throat and found himself saying, "I'm Jim, and I was laid off too. Bank-downsizing. Got two sons to feed. Thanks for the help." The two men shook hands, and Jim walked out of the food bank with a sack of groceries that morning, including some healthy breakfast cereals, bread, peanut butter, mayonnaise, sandwich meat, apples, canned baked beans, macaroni cheese mixes, orange juice, and milk. His step felt a little lighter, life a bit simpler, and he had enough food for a few days.

Questions for Personal Reflection and Group Discussion

1. In what ways are you aware of having too much? of needing to downsize because of moving, retiring, or simply because the spaces in the house are overly full?

2. How have you responded; sought to do something to lessen the amount of clutter?

3. In what way are you facing need, the need of not enough? In what way is life complicated by the daily grind of work—working two or three jobs, or trying to find a new job?

4. How do you find that the daily grind frustrates you—robs you of joy, energy, and being able to be simply present to yourself, your family, to the little things in creation and life around you?

5. As you get in touch with your inner and outer world, what voices are you becoming aware of?

A PERVASIVE LITANY

However, before we begin to think we are totally responsible for this overload, it is helpful to become aware of another subtle but ever-present message: the voice of the consumer world that "sings" to us as we shop. Its litany is artfully scripted. Hidden behind the well-organized and attractive rows of items in the stores, another intention is at work. Large sales companies spend huge sums of money studying our tastes, trends, desires, fears, and anxieties, and then plan their advertisements and sales methods accordingly. Store owners know that although customers enter their store with a prescribed list, seventy-five percent of what they actually purchase is spontaneous buying, prompted by the enticing way the store is arranged and where the advertised sale items are placed. The intention is that we will buy more of what we like or what we are told we need in order to....The lure of this voice is palpable.

The litany of the consumer world also is designed to work its way into a cultural level of anxiety within us. This voice reminds us that we need to have an attractive table setting; acceptable clothes to wear for work, for pleasure, for special occasions; the right hairstyle—along with the right shampoo, conditioner, and hairspray—so that we will feel that we, personally, will be in or will be enough. And while we are at it, the right vehicle and the right tools. Otherwise, we won't be in, won't have the latest look, and won't possess a green lawn or the kind of space, peace, and even the promise of retreat and freedom that the voice of the auto world promises if we purchase their latest design.

If we are finding ourselves facing the challenges of not having enough—money, work, food, health care, time, energy—then the lure of the consumer economy can trick us into buying what we cannot afford or frustrate us with its insinuation that we aren't able, we are not enough if we cannot afford to buy. We are not in.

When I was thirteen, my family was caught in the crisis of divorce. In the process, my mother and the four children found ourselves in need of a place to live, and my mom needed a place to work. My eldest brother went to live elsewhere and found a job. Our youngest brother was still with our dad. Money was tight, and there were many times when, as children, we asked about having something. The answer was, "No, we can't do that right now." Since I grew up in England, the public school system required that students wear a school uniform. Each school had its own design. I found myself having to wear the same school uniform in winter and summer, and when we moved and I switched schools, I did not have the right kind of uniform there either. At times, I felt embarrassed because I wasn't in.

However, at the same time, we learned the value of money—and learned to save our pennies—so that when special days came (birthdays, Easter, Christmas), we had enough to buy small gifts for one another. And when we did finally move into a little house my mother could afford (with some help from her brother), we were ecstatic, even as we entered the door and our few pieces of furniture were in disarray and nothing was unpacked. My eldest brother also returned home. I will never forget the beauty and joy of that moment.

Over the years that followed, I had more to learn: about economizing when planning meals, when needing new clothes (as children, we were all growing), when wanting to go somewhere in town. We walked a lot. And I finally saved up enough money to purchase a bike I could ride. We also enjoyed walks and picnics in places that were free of charge. It did not diminish the hours Mom worked or the attention we needed to give to budgeting, but the growing freedom which emerged as we learned how to manage with little is a gift and a skill that guides me through life.

We found ourselves out of step with the consumer world in many ways. And later, as each of us grew up and entered into the adult world of work, money, possessions, and what is in, we found ourselves also needing to reconfigure what true values are. The world's values and its litanies sing loud, making sure we are aware of trends.

Rita and her husband, Ralph, moved to Florida from New York state in order to find work and live in a warmer climate. But the jobs did not show up as promised, and Ralph, though working part-time here and there, began to despair of finding a full-time job driving trucks. Their savings were used up, and they wondered what to do. Finally, they decided to move close to a cousin in Virginia, and Ralph was able to find a full-time job driving trucks. Rita also began providing childcare. For a while, all seemed to be moving on the upswing, but then Rita began to have severe stomach problems and found she could not work. Because Ralph's work provided health insurance, she was covered when she found herself being referred to one doctor's office after another. After two years, she was faced with needing surgery. At this point, Ralph's company abruptly fired him. Health insurance vanished. Income stopped. While looking for other work, their vehicle broke down, and they discovered they needed a new engine.

In the mix of these years in Virginia, Rita had begun to attend a neighborhood Bible study held weekly in the home of a married couple now retired from decades of missionary work overseas. Ben and Daphne—kind, quiet-spoken, and hospitable—walked alongside Rita and Ralph through these trying months and years. Rita began to attend the church where Ben and Daphne were members, but Ralph was not about to join her. He had been publicly criticized and falsely condemned by a minister in another congregation a few years before, and Ralph had given up on church and felt distant from God.

Rita, now with no insurance coverage, was finally informed she would be able to receive free health coverage at a university hospital in Virginia. Within weeks, she was under the care of the head of the gastroenterology department and learned that a medical prescription would care for her stomach ailment; surgery was not needed. When a few folks in the congregation heard about the need of a new car engine, the funds were brought together. And in less than a week, Ralph was able to drive to begin looking for work again.

In the complicated mix of their life experience over those few years, this gift of presence, of being heard, and of help—the gifts of relationship where persons are accepted—smoothed the rough places in the road. And life became simpler again. There was enough, and they found themselves respected and cared for in the community of the congregation.

Questions for Personal Reflection and Group Discussion

1. As you reflect on the following questions and jot some notes of response in your journal, in what way are you becoming aware of the world's "voices"?

2. Pay attention to commercials—on TV, your computer, your smartphone or tablet—regarding car sales, hair products, diet plans, and so forth. Notice what they promise if you buy this product. They promise—in word, song, and picture— something you desire that is pleasurable. But, in fact, they are wanting you to buy their product.

3. In what way do your find yourself becoming hooked by commercial offers or by the way stores arrange and advertise their products? What helps you unhook?

4. Is there a time in your life when life experience caused sudden loss of place, income, or community? What gifts came toward you over that time? How did you find yourself reacting to being needy, not being in?

5. In what way can the church become a haven of care and help?

MONEY AND POSSESSIONS

While preparing a house for sale, we are told the house must be clean, including windows and bathrooms and kitchen. A freshly painted living room is also helpful (the new and in color is "greige": re-do your living room in that color!), along with attending to the landscaping, which will add value to the house. Translate that into: you can sell it for more.

Money is a major issue in our present world's economy. The present imbalance between the very wealthy and the middle- to lower-working-class grows each year. The price of groceries, health insurance, and prescription costs, along with the growing cost of rent or the mortgage payment on the house, and the cost of car payments and insurance, all place a major strain on the amount of income earned. Purchasing a new car is another issue. Most couples work full-time, and sometimes at more than one job. Otherwise, there is never enough. At the same time, we continue to shop and accumulate. Even those who invest in stocks, property, bonds, and other investments grow wealthier and wealthier but are never satisfied.

Money and possessions have a voice of their own. Whether we strain to make ends meet or strain to make even more on the stock market, the lure—like a flashing yellow light—signals its message: "If only we had more. . . ." As we become aware of the many voices that beckon, cajole, lure our attention, we may well ask, "How on earth can a person find any kind of simplicity in the world as it is?"

Thus, a move toward simplicity can also become complicated. If we do get rid of the clutter, the committee of voices within the commercial world will both sing us a song of having open space and joy, yet offer us many other things that will assure us of being with it or in. The voice of money will lure and cajole us one way or another with its message: "There is never enough."

And for some of us, that is how life is. There *is* never enough! And it is not the voice of the world speaking. Never enough is reality.

When our family was in transition between ministry assignments, my husband and I were looking for other employment. Ed decided to open his own painting/interior decorating business, but we had also just moved and did not have a base of persons we knew. We had some savings to fall back on, but rent and utilities and the usual needful expenses would soon eat away at what we had put aside. There would not be enough.

And then, to our surprise, when we attended the adult Sunday school class on the second Sunday of visiting the Mennonite church in a city south of us, the pastor who taught the class leaned back in his chair and said, "Now, we've studied the lesson and paid attention to how followers of Jesus in the church are to help each other when in need. How can we put this into action? We have a brother here who is needing work; what can we do about it?"

Never in my life had a minister made a public announcement about a church member or a person attending needing work. I was both embarrassed and shocked. Ed and I had lived this way: helping persons who were passing through the city where we were involved in youth missions, giving them a place to sleep for a few nights, and offering them meals. Or, inviting a man over for dinner and listening to his story of being in the process of settling in the United States for the first time and needing to find work before his wife and family came over. Or, giving hospitality for a few nights to a visitor from a Communist country who came to the West occasionally and just needed a place to stay while he connected with various persons in ministry in the area.

But now, here I sat, waking up to the reality that Ed and I were attending a congregation whose life together included practicing this kind of presence and hospitality to strangers like ourselves! Three men in the class leaned forward and mentioned work that each of them needed done and asked Ed to help. There would be some income while Ed built up the painting business. There would be enough. We were not seen and labeled as strangers, but as brother and sister in Christ and members of God's family.

In addition, for the first year as Ed developed the painting business, when I arrived home from teaching remedial math at the local grade school, I would find a sack full of groceries sitting beside our front door, once a week. We never found out who came and left this needed and much-appreciated gift of food by our door. But we did know that within this congregation, there were persons who lived out the ways of Jesus, caring for the needy and the poor. This is all part of the way in which simplicity is deeply embedded within relationship—relationship with God and with one another. We figure out ways to assure that each person, each family, has enough.

It was also during that season in the life of our family that Ed and I made a brave and, what felt like, risky decision: to raise quite significantly the amount of allowance our children would receive—especially as they entered their teen years. This was with the understanding that they would now be engaged in some kind of part-time work (babysitting, lawn-mowing, helping their dad paint, and so forth). They would also then be responsible for buying their own school supplies and their own clothes. We also assisted each of them in opening a bank account and working with savings, giving to the church, managing a debit card and cash flow, and so forth.

What our children discovered was that now they had choices as they learned to budget their spending, their savings, and their giving. After the first experience of going to town to purchase school clothes under this new arrangement, they talked about how they were now aware of the price of blue jeans and other clothing items.

"I looked first at the jeans I always wanted, but when I saw the price, I decided I didn't want them after all. I found some I really like for a fourth of the cost. Same with sneakers," remarked one of our teenage sons, now in high school.

The pathway to simplicity calls us to recognize the pervasive hold that money has on us and, in that recognizing, to pay attention to our own history of money. Our family of origin, along with the culture we grow up in, shapes our values and how we see the world around us, including how we relate to money. Since simplicity is embedded in freedom and in the reality of having enough, we pay attention to how this freedom, this having enough, emerges. And with it, how we can become freed from the lure and hold of money.

Questions for Personal Reflection and Group Discussion

1. As you think back on your childhood, what do you remember about money?

2. How was money talked about in your family?

3. What were the feelings around money?

4. What were you taught about money?

5. In your youth and young adult life, how did you relate to money? When you started working and earning money?

6. What were your hopes regarding money?

7. As an adult, in what ways has your attitude toward and use of money changed?

8. How much of a hold does money have on you? What helps you toward freedom from that control?

MORE VOICES: KEEP BUSY

In this twenty-first century, there is another committee of voices singing their song between the pages of our datebook—either paper or electronic— as we do our work on a project that is due and keep those appointments on the calendar where we enter all of the activities for each family member. If we have children, there are parent-teacher conferences to keep, concerts to attend, sports activities to watch, and homework to tend to after we have picked our children up from piano or guitar lessons or from a play date at a favorite friend's house. Busy people are admired. Henri Nouwen also comments on our daily routine: "In general, we are very busy people. . . . Our calendars are filled with appointments, our days and weeks filled with engagements, and our years filled with plans and projects. There is seldom a period in which we do not know what to do."[3]

Somehow, these many inner and outer voices possess an authority of their own. We want to be noticed, accepted, loved, listened to, respected, and understood. This desire to be connected also shows up as we make phone calls, send emails, text a friend, send a message by Twitter, do the daily look at Facebook and make an entry. This deeply embedded desire for community is within us. If we take a few moments to be honest, we become aware that this desire can even drive us to do whatever it takes to be in.

However, there is another layer of busy that is prevalent in our culture: the need to work three jobs in order to pay the mortgage, the car payment, health insurance, groceries, clothes, phone bills, and taxes. And a large percentage of families are provided for by one parent, with or without child support. Here, busy is not necessarily a desire to be in but to survive.

Another layer of busy presents itself as we listen to moms and dads who work long hours with little income: cleaning restrooms in the airport, cleaning rooms in motels, harvesting fruits and vegetables in the fields, serving as a checkout clerk in a grocery store, cleaning the floors and restrooms in the local school, working as a care assistant for the elderly and housebound, working in a fast food restaurant—doing labor-intensive work, but never earning enough. The wage scale is too low.

Where do we discover the path to simplicity among the many families who struggle to survive and among those whose work never provides enough?

Questions for Personal Reflection and Group Discussion

1. Reflect back over the past two weeks.

2. If you are working two or three jobs, begin to pay attention to:

    - Rhythm of work: In what way do you find joy or satisfaction in your work?

    - In what way does your work tire you?

3. Look at the spaces between working:

    - What kind of spaces are part of your week?

    - What fills those spaces at present?

    - As you look at the spaces a second (or third) time, how might one or two of those spaces become available for relaxation or play?

4. For what are you thankful?

5. If you are not working two or three jobs: look over the calendar or datebook where you jot down various appointments, meetings, and so forth. In what ways do you feel satisfied with the rhythm of the week? In what ways do you begin to feel like a taxi service or over-extended because of many appointments?

6. What voices drive your hectic schedule, your overly busy life?

RELATIONSHIP WITH OURSELVES: OUR BODIES ALSO SPEAK

At the same time, when we pause to breathe—to become conscious of the drive, the push, the stuff, the pace at which we live, the struggle to survive—we may find that the stress is invading our bodies. An inner form of messaging occurs; our bodies speak, desiring us to pay attention, to get the message. I was fixing dinner in the kitchen, fielding a phone call, and helping one of our children with their homework. At the same time, I was asking two of our other children to help with setting the table. Multitasking was something I did with ease, at least I thought I did. However, while tending to four things at once, I began to feel some stiffness and pain in the back of my neck and radiating down to my right shoulder. *Oh,* I thought, *my mom used to get a stiff neck all the time. I'll take some ibuprofen, and it'll go away.* I was not making any connection between the stress of multitasking and what my body was beginning to tell me.

But later that evening, some kinder voices entered into my inner conversation. I had attended a conference for pastoral caregivers a few months before, and the main speaker was a stress specialist. For the first time in my life, I became aware of how my body was carrying tension and, at times, letting me know about it. My hands would get cold; my neck would get stiff and would hurt. All stress messages. In the quiet of the evening, just before bed, I remembered

the speaker explaining how our bodies carry stress:
that which is too much for our souls to carry. And our
bodies will let us know—will speak to us. I rubbed my
neck and shoulder and sensed my body was speaking
to me. For the first time in my life, I was beginning
to listen to my body's voice. I was moving toward
relationship with myself, especially my body.[4]

My mother had always moved fast—whether
washing dishes, folding clothes, or cleaning house.
I had learned "fast" from her, and that gave rise to
multitasking. When I finally began to listen to my
body—this "friend" that would "never leave (me)"
and who "will be with (me) after death as (my) risen
companion of clearer light and swifter energy in a
different form"—and what this friend was telling me,[5]
I began responding with kindness: breathing slowly
in and out and releasing any tension throughout my
body. In time, the stiff necks and headaches ceased. I
slowed down.

When teaching a class in spiritual direction several
years ago, I invited the class members, who were
mostly clergy and actively engaged in congregational
ministry, to envision a ministry practice which would
care for the spiritual formation of persons in their
parish. One of the class participants was a single
woman who ministered in an inner-city church where
most of the members were employed and worked in
service stations, cleaning houses, as custodians in the
local school, and cleaning in the hospital.

Marcia found herself reflecting on the stress of life and how it affected the body. In time, she discerned that a way to tend to the spiritual as well as the physical needs of persons in the congregation would be to offer an after-work gathering. She invited anyone who was interested to stop in at the church for a half hour of "Rest, Relaxation, and God" (RR&G). Beginning at 5:30 p.m. as the folks made their way into the fellowship hall, Marcia said a few words of welcome, then invited those present to share their names and why they had decided to try out RR&G. Marcia also invited them to reflect on the work they did across the day and anything tough they were dealing with in their lives. Participants were then invited to lie down on a rug provided.

"Now it's time for you to rest, for fifteen minutes— to lay your body down on one of the rugs and to let God hold what's tough in your life as you rest. Jesus says, 'Come to me, all you who are carrying heavy loads, and I will give you rest.' So, do the comin' and the layin' down and rest. There'll be some quiet gospel music to help you relax." Marcia reminded the group that all they needed to do was rest and let Jesus hold anything that was stressful in the day.

Following the period of rest, Marcia asked folks to take a seat in the half circle of chairs, and to meet up two-by-two and share what the rest was like for their body, and to share what letting go was tough or heavy and letting God hold it was like. After the sharing, the group sang a simple gospel song together and closed with a benediction. She told the group that the fellowship hall would be open Monday through Friday from 5:30 to 6:00 p.m. for Rest, Relaxation, and God. No charge. They could come once, three times, or five days a week, whenever they wanted.

Marcia shared that this simple offering of the gift of being heard—being with a group of folks who worked, faced challenges of finances and other economic and family and cultural stressors, being offered a place to rest and lean into God—became life-giving and healing. The circumstances did not change, but the folks found they changed. And in time, some of them felt the call to be more involved in the church food bank, some with the childcare center, and some in the cultural care of the neighborhood, both in the school and in the city. A simplicity was emerging within and among them as these folks began to listen to their bodies and their lives, and as they learned to release what was tough or heavy into the greater holding of God.

Questions for Personal Reflection and Group Discussion

1. When are the moments when you wish for less rush, less anxiety, being less driven?

2. In what way might your body's voice be speaking to you, giving you tension signals?

3. What do you hear as you listen to the chorus of inner and outer voices challenging your desire, and what changes might you consider toward slowing down, discovering a different pathway in the world as it is?

4. What do you want?

5. What **do** you want?

6. What do you **really need**?

7. You may find it helpful to draw a picture of yourself, standing (or sitting).

   • On one side of your self-portrait, write your deeper desires—what you really want.

   • On the other side, write down what the chorus of inner and outer voices say—the voices that challenge your desires for change, something more spacious, restful.

CHAPTER 2
Pruning

You have heard that it was said . . .
but I say to you . . .
Blessed are the pure in heart, for they
will see God. (Matthew 5:21, 22, 8)

PRUNING

While we are learning how to collect, sort through, and (with kind attention) decide which items to keep and which items to pass on, we are in the process of pruning. If we are beginning to pay attention to the kind of stress we are carrying because of too much work and too little income, and we are seeking a different way forward, we are also in a process of pruning.

Orie Roth, a retired farmer in Iowa, came by our house in the late fall of our first year there. We had a grape arbor in the backyard, and he offered to prune it for us. We were grateful. Neither Ed nor I had any experience of tending grapevines. Orie went to work while I was folding laundry in the house and, when done, he came and knocked on the back door. "All done!" he said with a smile. I walked with him outside to see the results and, to my utter shock, all I could see were the curvy gray-brown main trunks of the vines, with very short stumps—really short—knotting the surface of the vines. He saw my face and said kindly, "That's what pruning is about. Thinning it all out is what helps the whole vine rest across the winter. This promotes fuller growth in the spring and a full harvest of grapes in the fall. You'll see." And I did. The following spring, the bare vine and short stumps came alive with green shoots, new branches, blooms in the late summer, and an abundant harvest of grapes in the fall. Orie's wisdom, which grew out of his experience, held true. Hence, sorting through the many items which have been living in one's house for years is like pruning, kind of cutting back, but with good results in mind.

There is also the inner pathway to tend. Here, we discover that a kind of pruning also needs to be done. Thankfully, Jesus doesn't walk off and leave us to figure all that out on our own. Like Orie, Jesus comes and not only points out what areas we need to tend, but stays to help with the work. Eugene Peterson is well-aware that in our technological culture, we are trained for doing and getting, producing and accumulating. However, the pathway to simplicity calls us to being and becoming. Peterson writes,

> We are accustomed to think of our age as conspicuously technological. But the largest area of the human continent is impoverished . . . the vast interiors are bereft. The consequence is that . . . most people don't

venture into these interiors, at least not very far.[1]

Hence, Jesus' emphasis on charting a path into the interior and offering guidance for the inner pathway. In his desire to give the multitude and his close disciples guidance for turning to walk that inner path, he climbs up a nearby mountainside, then sits down—a signal in his culture that he was about to teach or preach.

PRUNING OUR ASSUMPTIONS ABOUT WEALTH, POWER, AND ACCEPTANCE

Rather than beginning by pumping people up, making them feel good about themselves, and promising ways to success and economic wealth, Jesus starts out by being honest about what we experience in those times when we feel that hunger to come home to God. Ever since Eden, we have been caught in this painful quandary between desiring to be in relationship with God and being afraid of even coming close because we can never be enough. We feel guilt and shame. Jesus begins by offering a gentle pathway into our inner poverty and fear by saying,

Blessed are the poor in spirit,
for theirs is the kingdom of heaven.
(Matthew 5:3)

When Jesus looks out over the crowd, he knows that so many of these men and women are physically and economically poor and, at the same time, are coming close because deep within them, they are feeling their own sense of need to be in relationship with God. Jesus has compassion on the crowd, aware of how harassed and lost people are, like sheep without a shepherd (Matthew 9:35-36). And so, he begins his teaching by giving a blessing: "Blessed are the poor in spirit, for theirs is the kingdom of heaven" (Matthew 5:3).

What Jesus is saying is that the very feeling of being unable, unworthy, not measuring up is a doorway into blessing: the blessing of being accepted in the great realm of God's care. When Jesus declares that the poor in spirit are blessed, he is not saying, "If you will, then . . ." The blessing is unconditional. The blessing is free, a gift. The blessing brings into being what it says. There is a transformative movement here which God works within us. We find ourselves experiencing the joy of being welcomed and accepted, even as we know we are unable, dependent, needy, even guilty, and lost.

"Poor" also speaks of an additional truth and realization. It is one thing to read a truth; it is another to experience the truth within. In this case, "poor" means we are dependent on God for everything:

Our creation: we did not create ourselves;
Who we are: beloved persons created in
God's image: naked and
provided for, and in community;
The very breath we breathe;
The food God has created and provides for

us to eat;
The earth itself;
The community of humankind created in
God's image;
all held within the loving and blessed
purposes of God, to which
God comes among us, in relationship.
(See Genesis, chapters 1 and 2.)

We discover this coming of God among us threaded all through the Scriptures, from Genesis onward. And in Jesus, God comes among us in person and moves into our neighborhood. At Pentecost, the Holy Spirit comes and dwells within and among us, signaling God-with-us-always.

Further on in his mountainside teaching, Jesus makes a distinction between what the Law[2] says and what he is saying. The Law lays out the rules and then gives the list of punishments for breaking the rules. Only in being obedient to the Law does one become righteous and acceptable. Jesus looks back at the Law and says, "You have heard it said," but then goes on to say, "but I say unto you." (See Matthew 5:2-22, 27-28, 31-34.) Rather than being met by a list of rules and punishments for offenses, we are met with a call to a deeper look at our heart and its intentions, along with mercy, kindness, and provision. (See Matthew 6:25-34.) Jesus speaks gospel, not law: good news for all those who come. Hence, Jesus is offering us a window into the core of who he is and what he is about to teach throughout this mountain message.[3]

There is a philosophy within our modern/
postmodern era: life only happens if we make it
happen. It is all up to us. But this is false. Rather, we
respond to being in this world—being created and
being sustained by God. God is the Great Initiator.
Our response, then, shapes the way we and others
relate to one another and how we experience life
in this world. This side of Eden, we tend to sideline
God. But God in grace and kindness keeps coming,
seeking to awaken us to the reality of being created
in relationship, God included—even God foremost.
Thus, the person, the community who is poor in
spirit, is awakening to this grace and sustenance God
gives. And in this awakening comes awareness of
dependency. We don't have to navigate life alone.

The world does not see this truth, does not offer
grace and gift, but drags us into seeing ourselves
through the eyes of others: judged, labeled, reacted
to. We may well ask, *Who is in charge? What governs
or controls the relationship? What force or impulse is at
work here?* As followers of Jesus, we are called and
companioned to be in the world but not to be of the
world—not to be run around and controlled by the
world's ways of seeing and doing—the world's ways
of figuring out what it takes to make us, you and me,
"somebody."

Hence, when we find ourselves lacking in
comparison with what the world wants and sees us
to be; when we feel less than, poor, insufficient; Jesus
says,

*Blessed are the poor in spirit, for theirs is
the kingdom of heaven.
(Matthew 5:3)*

And then there is also the deep, grinding reality
of being poor: not enough provision for food, shelter,
medical care, clothes, children's education, money to
fix the car or even to buy a car! Even public education
costs. I remember when Ed was building up his
painting business and how tight our income was. As
the children were about to leave the house for school,
each one needed money for a gift for the teacher's
aide who was done with her time and two dollars
toward the expenses of a field trip the following day.
And so, the requests came. As a child, I had been told
no so many times, I had decided not to say no to our
children. But as I gave each child what they asked for,
I was mentally counting in my head how much I had
left for other household expenses, including paying the
monthly electric bill, groceries, and gas.

Jesus had deep compassion on the multitude of
people who were poor. So, also, did John the Baptist.
As John prepared the people for the coming of this
One, the people asked how they could prepare
themselves. John said, "Whoever has two coats must
share with anyone who has none; and whoever has
food must do likewise" (Luke 3:11). While we may
feel humiliated and "less than" if we accept such
"handouts," Jesus assures us we are enough. We are
beloved. Our very neediness places us in line with all
those who God sees, cares for, and calls to help each

other. In this way, we become the family, the "body" of Jesus, so that no one goes in need. We are learning to love our neighbor as we love our self. In the Book of Acts, we discover that those who chose to follow the way of Jesus

> *had all things in common; they would sell*
> *their possessions and goods*
> *and distribute the proceeds to all, as any*
> *had need. . . . There was not a*
> *needy person among them.*
> *(Acts 2:44b-45; 4:34a)*

I also needed to learn how to make ends meet. Thus, I discovered over time to pay attention to consignment stores—wonderful places to find clothes for the children; to those days when a local Christian school offered a "Trash and Treasure Day," raising money for the school, but at the same time offering all manner of goods, including children's clothes, toys, kitchen appliances, and so forth, at a low price we could afford. When accompanying a woman who was unable to work because of multiple illnesses and who was on Medicaid, I learned more about agencies that are helpful: the electric company offered help to those who could not afford to pay their heat bill or their cooling bill. I discovered that Social Services puts families in touch with funds to assist low-income parents, subsidized rent, jobs, and help with transportation. A group of lawyers offered free legal care once a year to persons earning less than a certain amount. Congregations often offer community meals once a month or even once a week, and have a giveaway "shop" where families can come and find what they need. One congregation opened a "free" school shop that had all of the required school supplies for the students in a local grade school, with the invitation to come and shop at the beginning of each school term. In this way, we find that we are not alone. Life becomes simpler.

Questions for Personal Reflection and Group Discussion

1. In what way(s) are you aware of times when you wondered if God would find you acceptable?

2. As you get in touch with Jesus saying, "Blessed are the poor in spirit, for theirs is the kingdom of heaven," in what ways do you feel poor?

   In relation to the world around you:
   physically
   economically
   socially

   In relation to God:
   unworthy
   unacceptable

3. As you listen to Jesus giving you a blessing as a person who is poor, what do you notice?

PRUNING: AWAKENING US TO OUR DIVIDED AND
DISTRACTED LOYALTIES

A little later in this mountain sermon, Jesus speaks
another blessing:

> *Blessed are the pure in heart, for they will*
> *see God. (Matthew 5:8)*

Here, Jesus is laying out the pathway to simplicity.
Here, "pure" means a single-minded devotion to God,
an undivided heart. The psalmist is also aware that
we need God to teach us, to help us know, and to
help us walk in God's ways. And beyond this, it is God
who gives us an undivided heart, not something we
accomplish by ourselves (Psalm 86:11).[4] Rather than
dividing our loyalties between competing voices, our
devotion to God becomes the sphere within which all
other people, all things, take their rightful place.

During this journey of pruning, of choosing to take
off the old and put on the new, of choosing to die to
the old nature and its insistent voices, and to follow
the leading of the Holy Spirit (Colossians 3:12-17),
we begin to notice how our attitude is changing. We
awaken to how short-tempered we are when our turf
(from our perspective) is invaded, how self-serving we
are when things don't go our way and we complain,
how attached we are to the way the culture demands
our loyalty at Thanksgiving or Christmas. And when
we do choose change, we do the hard work of ceasing
to react the way we did and gradually develop a new,
life-giving habit of kindness and patience.

In time, in God's time, we will become aware that God is doing a deeper un-muddying of the source, a work that we cannot do on our own. God is always about creating an uncluttered heart within us, that essential center of who we are. Thus, as we tend the outward things on our way to outward simplicity, we will discover we are called to work at the inward pruning. God is the great Vine Grower who is also at work, pruning back those things within us that block and hinder our freedom.

SEASONS FOR PRUNING

Just as Orie came knocking on our door in the fall to prune the grapevines, so letting go of the old and making room for the new can have its seasons. In the midst of it all, we are learning to pay attention to:

Letting go of	Making room for
Attachment	Letting go
Worry that triggers distractions	Presence and hospitality
False voices	Hearing the true voice
Accumulation, "taking"	Being present, receiving
The limitations of old stories	Freedom of new stories
Taking off . . .	Putting on . . .

When Moving from Your Home

When we moved from Virginia to Texas, we were surprised at how many books we owned: Ed's pastoral library, my teaching library, our home library—including the children's favorite books. For us, books are like friends. And more than that, they take us to another world when we read. One of our grandsons was talking about his love for books, especially books about dinosaurs. He was eleven at the time.

"Grandma, when I read about dinosaurs, I like to go back in time and find myself there where they are—tall and way above me. It's fantastic! And then, if it gets scary, I can just come back to where I am and the dinosaurs stay back there."

"Still in the book!" I replied.

"Yes. Books are great like that."

Thus, simplifying for us included coming to terms with our passion for books.

However, we began to realize that what we love can become an "attachment," and we came closer to the reality that behind the pull of attachment lives the lure of addiction. We were more addicted to these books than we realized—and this addiction lured us away from further sorting of the books, along with boxing them up and finding other persons, places, and worthy causes to donate them to.

To help me get in touch with what was happening, I spent time in God's presence and, after confessing the fix I found myself in, I waited. God showed me that it wasn't just the books; it was also the file folders and articles, course materials, writings that I had prepared across three decades of teaching, giving spiritual direction, and giving supervision. I heard

God say, "Go through one box a time, keep what is helpful, and return the rest to the earth: allow the rest to be shredded by a company that cares for the environment."

We are more addicted in our society than we care to admit: to things; to being busy; and to accumulating, producing, and being in constant motion. We are also glued to our belief that these things are what it takes to be in and make us somebody. So sings the final stanza of the Western economy's litany.

We learn as we go—as did those early disciples. Aware of the many voices which seek to dominate our life in service of the false self, Jesus continues to open up the pathway inward as he says, "For those who want to save their life will lose it, and those who lose their life for my sake will find it. For what will it profit them if they gain the whole world but forfeit their life?" (Matthew 16:25-26a). When Jesus speaks of the life we want to save, he is directing our attention to the self which we allow the world's system to form: the false self. Paul, in his letter to the believers in Rome— capital of the Roman Empire—calls them to "not be conformed to this world, but be transformed by the renewing of your minds, so that you may discern what is the will of God—what is good and acceptable and perfect" (Romans 12:2). Movement in the direction of this inward path takes some serious pruning, a sacrificial offering to God: a giving up of our love and attachment to the things of this world. In his letter to the believers in Colossae, Paul also writes about pruning, taking off the old and putting on the new (Colossians 3:12-14).

Questions for Personal Reflection and Group Discussion

1. As you begin to attend to one or two areas in your house or your life, in order to prune—to be thankful for the gift which this item has meant in your life and then to let it go—in what ways are you feeling the tug of attachment?

2. Do you sometimes find that you avoid getting back into dealing with the clutter or sorting through those things which have been stored or piled somewhere? What might be behind that resistance?

3. What helps you get back into the task? What brings you joy as you continue?

4. What helps you let go?

Moving to a Retirement Home

We were renting a house in the country, about a mile from town, and at the same time looking forward to finding a more permanent home. The son of the owner of the property had become engaged and, after his marriage, would be moving into the house we were renting.

While attending the monthly gathering of the quilters' group and observing the women as they leaned into that practiced, fine hand-stitching of colorful and artfully pieced quilting tops, I had been invited to bring the devotional. While reflecting on the season of life in which most of the women found themselves, I became aware of what it meant for each of these faithful women to make that final move. First, a move from the farm to living in town. Then, a move to the retirement home. This last move would be a decisive one: a signal of age, of facing into the final years and letting go of so much that one had accumulated over the last decades. So, I told a story of Sadie, who was sorting through her many things and choosing those few things she would be able to house in a small retirement apartment across the road from her house. Her daughter, Anna, called on the phone, a bit anxious that Sadie was taking too much time deciding. Anna reminded Sadie that they needed to be at the retirement home by 3:00 p.m. that day. Sadie also found herself anxious. It wasn't so much the sorting and packing; it was the reality of it all. Albert had died five years before, and usually he would be her ballast: the steady presence who did the heavy lifting. But Albert had gone on ahead of her through the portals of death into heaven, and she would need to make this final move on her own. She found herself gazing out of the window, feeling pensive and needy. After a few minutes, a red cardinal flew to the bird feeder and perched, holding still before pecking into the birdseed. It was March; spring was barely present. The shrubs and trees were still empty, waiting for warmth and life to return. But as the cardinal sat on the edge of the feeder, Sadie felt a warmth in her soul. It was as if God had sent a gift. The cardinal was Albert's favorite bird. He always knew when spring would finally come because the cardinals began to visit their bird feeders. She smiled and felt a presence within and around her as she prepared to cross the street into this final move in life. She looked at the clock, 12:00 p.m. Time for lunch, and then she would finish the packing. The clock would also need to be packed.

As I told the story, I was aware of the way in which its gentle reality touched the souls of the women. Phoebe was sitting at the end of one of the long quilting frames and, as I walked back to sit down, she reached out and touched my arm. I stood still and turned toward her. Her blue eyes looked up at me through her silver-rimmed glasses and she said, "I'm going to be moving soon—across the street, the home. And my house; I won't need it anymore. Do you have a house yet?"

"No, Phoebe, not yet," I replied.

"Then maybe you and your husband and family would like to have mine. Would you like to come over soon and take a look?"

"Phoebe, we would love to come. Thank you so much for thinking of us. We are in need of a place."

And so, finally, the moving day came. And as we walked into the house, there was Phoebe, sitting at the kitchen table, sorting through a shoebox brimming full of old letters, carefully arranged in their envelopes, complete with addresses and the stamps of other countries and decades past. Phoebe was figuring out which grandchild, which great-grandchild, which niece or nephew would receive each one of these envelopes which housed letters containing memories of life in Switzerland and Alsace-Lorraine (in France, also once part of Germany), gems from the past. Her two daughters were standing nearby, anxious about the length of time Sadie was taking to sort and decide.

"Please, don't worry," we said. "Sadie, take all the time you need. We are not in a hurry. We can even finish the move tomorrow if needed. Those letters are precious, important pieces of your own story that you want to pass on and be known and held."

Thus, moving to a retirement home has its own season of pruning, remembering, holding, sifting, passing on pieces of stories to be held, and knowing that one is also held in the care of family and of God— and God's great story that holds all of ours.

When Feeling Worried, Inadequate, Distracted

Following the awakening—when we become aware that we would like to, and even need to, set out on this journey: this pilgrimage of sorting, sifting, and pruning—we discover that as we get to the work of actually doing, the inner journey claims our attention, sometimes with joy and sometimes with frustration, even avoidance. How we feel counts. How we feel can also color how we think. Beyond our thoughts, how we feel can trigger the voices of the committee of selves within. Before we get hard on ourselves and tell ourselves just to "Get over that kind of stuff!" let's turn to a story in the Great Story and see what we can discover there.

The story we are turning to takes us to the front door of a house in Bethany, a town close to Jerusalem. Jesus has just arrived at the door, along with his disciples. We join them as they knock at the door. This cluster of visitors has walked far—some, one hundred miles—from the Hermon mountain range north of Capernaum on the north shore of the Lake of Galilee. They are on their way to Jerusalem to celebrate the Passover, that meal which draws their memory and presence to be with the family of Jacob as God is standing vigil across the night, in order to free this nation from slavery in Egypt and to lead them to the land of promise.

Tired, feet dusty and worn, they wait. A woman opens the door and welcomes them in. This is Martha, who shares this house with her sister, Mary. We turn

now to Luke's Gospel, chapter 10, to read verses
38-42.

Pause for prayer before reading:

Open my eyes, Lord, and help me to see.

*Open the ears of mind and heart, and help me to
hear.*

*Just as Martha opened the door of her house to
you and your followers,*

*and to me, help me to open the door of my outer
world and my inner world, the world of my heart,
to you.*

*Help me to listen and truly hear what you say to
me.*

*For the sake of your loving purposes in the world.
Amen.*

Then turn to the Gospel narrative below.

*If you are engaging with this reading and reflection
with a group, invite persons in the group to volunteer to
read the various voices.*

Narrator

Martha

Mary (while Mary does not speak, her intention
and body language do speak)

Jesus

Narrator: Now as they went on their way, [Jesus]
entered a certain village, where a woman named
Martha welcomed him into her home. She had a sister
named Mary, who sat at the Lord's feet and listened to

what he was saying. But Martha was *distracted* by her many tasks; so she came to him and asked,

Martha: Lord, do you not care that my sister has left me to do all the work by myself? Tell her then to help me.

Jesus: Martha, Martha, *you are worried and distracted by many things;* there is need of only one thing. Mary has chosen the better part, which will not be taken away from her.

Pause in silence for two minutes.

Become aware of what you heard, what you noticed as you entered into Martha and Mary's house, and what you watched and listened to that was happening.

Now read this narrative again.

Questions for Personal Reflection and Group Discussion

1. What tends to distract you: pull you away from what you intend to do, hear, say? (Given, there are legitimate reasons we need to leave what we are doing and give our attention elsewhere. When our children were in preschool, they would come and pull on my sweater to get my attention, calling my name, "Mom! Mom!" Of course, they needed my full attention: body, mind, and eyes. Listening was paramount.)

2. What do you find yourself worrying about?

3. In what way do you find yourself becoming angry or sorry for yourself?

4. How do you tend to react to those around you? to the situation at hand?

5. What helps you "find your way home" to your true self and to those around you? to God?

OUR COMMITTEE OF SELVES: OTHER VOICES

As Martha, who has decided that she must serve more and therefore fix more, becomes more tense and then worried about how much there is to do, she begins to notice she is in the kitchen alone while her sister, Mary, is sitting—doing nothing from Martha's perspective—in the living room listening to Jesus. Now Martha becomes angry at the unfairness of it all. Doesn't Jesus see that she is on her own, doing all the work? Doesn't he care? He should. Martha's committee of selves has taken charge, pulling her away from being present to her innate gift of hospitality and the joy of being present for guests. Martha sees herself as unfairly overworked and driven by the many demands she is making on herself in order to feed and to please the guests in her house. Here, the compulsive voices take charge which run by the rules laid down by:

- *The perfectionist self,* who *fears* not living up to the standards and expectations of others; whose mantra is: make sure you make enough; prepare the dishes so that they measure up to cultural expectations; and make sure that the house is acceptable, tidy, and clean!

- *The victimized self,* who is not able to ask for what she needs.

- *The lonely, abandoned self,* who judges her sister, Mary, to have left her alone to do everything, and so feels sorry for herself.

- *The needy self,* who judges herself to be unnoticed and uncared for by Jesus. He is the one who cares for the needy, heals and tends the poor and sick. Why isn't he noticing her?

- *The angry and critical self,* who is reacting at her sister. Mary is not lifting a finger to help. This self is pushed by the injustice of being ignored.

- *The boss, the take-charge self,* now speaks, taking over the situation in order to put it right. This self questions Jesus, and then orders him to command Mary to help Martha.

But Jesus is not swayed by the questioning or the commands. He sees with kindness how the pain and worry which Martha carries distracts her in such a way that she becomes lost among the voices of her inner selves. With tenderness, he offers Martha a way back to herself. First, by calling her name, twice. He is inviting her to return from where she is kidnapped and come back home to her true self, into true community.

He gently directs her attention to what is needed, "There is need of only one thing." We might interpret that to mean that Martha only needs to prepare one dish, rather than so many. But Jesus is speaking to a deeper place within her. He is inviting Martha to a singleness of heart and soul—from the demands of the house of fear to the freedom of the house of love. In that house, she gathers her life and work around Jesus and his way of love, rather than being pulled around by the many selves and their fears and demands.

Mary is at rest. She has chosen to be present to her inner self and not be dragged into compulsive worry or be distracted by the voice of the false self. She has learned how to sit and listen to Jesus—to truly listen. As we sit on the mountainside along with Jesus, the crowd, and his disciples, notice how Jesus says:

Pay attention to how you listen. (Luke 8:18)

Questions for Personal Reflection and Group Discussion

1. Whom do you identify with in this story?

2. Where did you find yourself in Martha and Mary's house?

3. In what way do you identify with the many selves that tend to distract and distance us from our self and from others?

4. When you bring this into your prayer, what do you notice?

5. What is God's invitation to you?

6. In what way are you learning to listen to those around you? to your inner self/selves? to God?

CHAPTER 3
Illumination

Then turning toward the woman,
[Jesus] said to Simon, "Do you
see this woman?" (Luke 7:44)

Simplicity can have a number of meanings:

paring down	enough
plainness	simple beauty
unity	being in community
un-mixedness	pure, safe, not
oneness	contaminated
singleness	harmony
congruency	a safe center
integration	all the pieces work together
	all the pieces weave
	together

Take some time to jot down what thoughts come to mind as you read each of these words. Then reflect on what the word *simplicity* means for you. Share your thoughts with others in your group.

GOING DEEPER

I would like to draw our attention to the term
un-mixedness—not a word we use very much, maybe
not at all, but a term which can shed some light on
what we mean when we use the word *simplicity*.
So, to start with, what is in the "mix"? And what is
"mixedness"? I like to cook and am aware that the
ingredients I choose to place in the mixing bowl—
along with how much of each—are basic to preparing
food and to how the recipe turns out. I remember once
making the mistake of using baking soda instead of
sugar when making a cake. I stirred the baking soda
into the mix, and once I realized what I had done,
I knew I would need to start over. I was unable to
unmix what was already in the mixing bowl.

If we take that analogy further, there are
components of our lives that form part of the mix
of who we are and what we do. The question is:
Are the components (ingredients) in harmony with
each other? Do they belong? Or, do parts of the mix
fight each other, and so cause continual unrest and
tension? And once we get in touch with the mix within
us and desire that some of the ingredients need to
be let go, how do we arrive at un-mixedness? As I
learned while cooking, once all the ingredients are in
the bowl, we cannot unmix them, but we can choose
to start over. But unmixing ourselves is subtler and
needs more than "starting over." This is where we
need help from beyond ourselves, when it comes to
sorting out the "mix" within ourselves.

This side of Eden, all humankind is caught in the tension between the true, created self which is created in God's image and is enough, and the false adapted self which gathers its focus around protecting its self, serving its self. This is the mix we live with. The compulsive drive of the adapted self can cause us to be off-balance and to ignore the voice and presence of the deeper, truer self.

God is fully aware of our condition—the mix within us: both that which is good, whole, and enough; and that which contaminates the mix: the presence and drive of the adapted or false self[1], driven by the ways of the world and even evil itself. But God does not walk away, rather God comes to bring us to freedom: freedom from the pull of the false self and freedom from the damage that the adapted self manufactures within the mix of our lives. God comes to bring us back into harmony with God—to come home to God, to ourselves, to each other, and to the creation God provides for place, for sustenance, for beauty, and for our engagement in stewardship.

So, how does God help us to become aware? What kind of "texts" does our Creator send us? How does God draw us onto the inner pathway of un-mixedness, of simplicity? How God comes may not always be recognized. But be assured, God comes with gentleness, offering a blessing. Like a good shepherd, God comes to find what we have lost and cannot find within the world of our soul. We begin to see our lives differently; a clarity is given. How we see and relate to our life changes.

Some of the ways God comes to guide us onto the inner pathway can include

- passages of Scripture

- an eyes-open walk in creation

- drawing our awareness to see what is missing in the mix of our lives

- learning to see beyond the surface of the ordinary

- seeing as Jesus sees others in the world

- reflecting on how we see (discernment, consciousness examen)

God comes to bring clarity and guidance as we make choices, and there are many choices as we walk the inward and outward paths. In the process, we find that we are learning discernment—learning to notice the difference between what is of the false self and what is of the true self; what in the mix is life-giving and what is life-draining; what leads to tension and unrest; and what leads to the simplicity of living in harmony with God, with ourselves, and with others—and God's creation.

Passages of Scripture

Near the end of his life, Moses gathers the people and the leaders of Israel and speaks to them—offering them the choice between listening to God and following the way of God and blessing or listening to the many other voices that will lead them away from God and result in tension, war, loss, and robbery.

Saying yes to God draws them into the covenant God is making with them—not a legal covenant, but a relational covenant made in deep love and faithful commitment.[2] These people carry the blessing given to Abraham and Sarah to carry for the sake of the world (Genesis 12:1-2).

Joshua retells this story to the people now living in the land of promise, a land with fruit and vineyards they did not plant. He calls them to remember God, the LORD who had led them here:

> *Choose this day whom you will serve,*
> *whether the gods your ancestors served in*
> *the region beyond the River or the gods of*
> *the Amorites in whose land you are living;*
> *but as for me and my household, we will*
> *serve the LORD. (Joshua 4:15)*

In the Gospel narratives, we hear Jesus also calling his followers to choose:

> *If any want to become my followers, let*
> *them deny themselves (the false self) and*
> *take up their cross daily and follow me.*
> *For those who want to save their life will*
> *lose it (their false self), and those who lose*
> *their life (reject the voices of the false self*
> *and its manipulation) for my sake will save*
> *it (live into their true self as they follow*
> *Jesus). What does it profit them if they*
> *gain the whole world, but lose or forfeit*
> *themselves? (Luke 9:23-25,*
> *parentheses added)*

Here, we find Jesus bringing the false self and the true self into focus, along with the nature of the battle between the two: between what the false self wants and what the true self desires. He goes on to explain more fully what the wants of the false self look like: the false self is never satisfied, always seeks more. And so, Jesus brings into question what the person will gain, what profit they will obtain if they gain the whole world. If we finally own everything the world has to offer, Jesus says we will lose ourselves. We may own the whole world, but at the same time lose who we truly are. Finally, we lose. Jesus goes on to further clarify the struggle:

> *No one can serve two masters; for a slave*
> *will either hate the one and love the other,*
> *or be devoted to the one and despise the*
> *other. You cannot serve God and wealth*
> *(and all that obtaining wealth entails).*
> *(Matthew 6:24, parentheses added)*

We all give our lives to someone or something. And we serve what or who we give our lives to. Who or what is really in charge?

As we walk the path Jesus offers, we are on the pathway which beckons the true self to enter into the struggle of dying to the false, and thus do not lose who we truly are created in God's image. Our false self is always worried and stressed, especially about not having enough. The original lie spun in Eden is embedded in the DNA of our false self and continues to spin its web in the form of, "If you have . . . , then you will be . . ." There is no rest nor simplicity found here.

Aware of the mix of selves within us and how we tend to worry, Jesus offers us some gentle guidance: take an eyes-open walk in creation to truly see, and we will begin to see as Jesus sees—to know God's deep presence and care which stills the anxious voices of worry, demand, shame, and guilt.

Prayerful Practice: Taking a Walk Outside in Creation

Here, we discover the kind guidance Jesus offers in the midst of our anxiety and worry. He is inviting our attention to creation where, as we pause, gaze, and notice, we become aware of God's care. This is a call to stop, to contemplation. To gaze for a while—even ten to fifteen minutes. In this way, the tight grasp of the false self loosens its grip and control.

As you walk in creation, Jesus gives you guidance:

I tell you, do not worry about your life, what you will eat or what you will drink, or about your body, what you will wear. . . . Look at (open your eyes to see, contemplate) the birds of the air; they neither sow nor reap nor gather into barns, and yet your heavenly Father feeds them. Are you not of more value than they? And can any of you by worrying add a single hour to your span of life? And why do you worry about clothing? Consider (open your eyes to see, contemplate) the lilies of the

*field, how they grow; they neither toil nor
spin, yet I tell you, even Solomon in all his
glory was not clothed like one of these....
Therefore do not worry . . . strive first for
the kingdom of God and his righteousness,
and all these things will be given to you as
well. (Matthew 6:25-29, 31, 33,
parentheses added)*

Questions for Personal Reflection and Group Discussion

1. As you walk outside and pause to look (contemplate)—to gaze at the birds, the grasses, and the wildflowers—what do you notice?

2. How does the kind counsel of Jesus weave its way into what you see and how you are now seeing?

3. In what way are you becoming aware of God's care and provision?

SOMETHING MISSING IN THE MIX

Have you ever tried to make bread and forgot to add yeast? Or, tried to bake a cake and forgotten to add the rising agent? Once we realize what we have not done, we realize that something is missing. The result is a flat, hard bread or a cake that is dense and stodgy. Jesus picks up on this theme. Countless times, he had watched his mother, Mary, as she measured flour and kneaded in the yeast. This common, daily sustenance he kneads into his own storytelling:

> *The kingdom of heaven is like yeast that a woman took and mixed in with three measures of flour until all of it was leavened. (Matthew 13:33)*

Thus, as the ways and purposes of God enter more deeply, are kneaded into our being and our doing, there is transformation. The presence of God within us brings this transformative and life-giving change. This is the work of God's doing in and among us. As we lean into God's ways, God is at work in us. We are never the same—for our sake and for the sake of the world.

The Stock Market Investor and His Narrow World

Four-year-old Patty went to stay with her Uncle Matt for a few days. He lived in a high-rise apartment in the city and owned his own investment business. Patty soon realized that as she played quietly with her blocks, dolls, and picture books, her uncle sat in front of his computer most of the day—with short breaks for lunch and to fix dinner. In her little mind, she wondered why. On the third day, Patty wandered over to where he was sitting at his desk, examining the latest returns on a certain investment, and asked, "Uncle Matt, is that all you do?"

Her question alerted him to the reality that his niece was there standing beside him; but Patty's question also gave him pause. These five words coming from this little preschool girl began kneading themselves into a deeper place: the house of his soul, the interior of his person, his true being. And once there, this "yeast" created space for awareness. An awareness of his need for something more began to capture his attention. He had ignored and forgotten this inner realm, this seat of the true self. But now he was awake to what had been missing.

God's text had come tucked inside this child's question. Matt began to make plans to leave his business and to travel in order to find something more satisfying, something spiritual. This was what was missing from the mix within his life and work.

This hunger, this awareness that something is missing, alerts us to paying attention. We may try to feed that awareness that something is missing by going on a spending spree or engaging in any number of activities. But in our quieter moments, we realize that all these other things are not satisfying. There is something more, something deeper we need. We need to come home to God.

Questions for Personal Reflection and Group Discussion

1. So, it is in a multitude of ways that God comes and awakens our awareness that something is missing in the mix of our lives and that we need something more. As you read these narratives, what stands out for you?

2. In what way does it resonate with you?

3. In what way(s) are you aware of an event, a conversation, something you read or saw that touched on a deeper, internal awareness in your life?

4. What do you remember as that awareness came to the surface?

5. How did you stay to listen? to be present?

6. In what way was God at work in your life as you faced that awareness?

Seeing Beyond the Surface of the Ordinary: Dirty Dishes in the Mix

Janice and her husband, Max, lived on the north side of a college town, on a quiet street among some wealthy neighbors: a vice president of a major company in the United States, a top-ranked scientist who oversaw the workings of a nuclear experimental laboratory, the president of the college, a stockbroker who had made millions, among others. Janice enjoyed having neighbors in for our monthly potlucks, and she liked to keep a tidy house. When I dropped by to visit, Janice was in the kitchen putting breakfast dishes in the dishwasher after Max, a horticulturist, had left for work and their two grade-school daughters had left for school. I offered to help her clear the breakfast table, but Janice said, "Oh, no! Do take a seat in the living room. I don't want you to see the dirty dishes in the kitchen. I'll be right there!" Once she had brought her kitchen into immaculate order, Janice joined me in the living room. "Dirty dishes are such a problem," she said. "They make the kitchen look bad."

In the home of my childhood and teen years, dirty dishes weren't "bad," but they did have to be duly washed, dried, and put away. My mother washed the dishes at high speed, and we children learned to dry each cup, dish, and plate in haste. The reason? So that we could get to something else—something more agreeable, likable. Hence, the message was, "Washing dishes is needful, but not a job to be savored; rather it was kind of a necessary nuisance. So, wash and dry them as quick as you can, and then you can go do something you like to do."

Dirty dishes seemed to carry the brunt of standing in the way, a kind of obstacle to be taken care of. Janice could not give herself permission to sit down and visit until the dirty dishes were done. My mother— and we, her children—attacked the job of washing dishes with a view to "get that job done," so we could then be free to do something we liked to do.

It wasn't until some years later that I began to see dirty dishes through a different lens. Ed had left the house to work in his painting business, the children were all in school, and I decided to sit down in the kitchen for a few minutes before washing the breakfast dishes. We did not have a dishwasher at that time. As I sat, I began gazing at the stack of cereal bowls, plates, cups, and juice and milk glasses, and it occurred to me that forty minutes ago, these same dishes were completely acceptable: first sitting clean and arranged in the familiar pattern around the table, ready for breakfast. And then, also quite acceptable, these same bowls held cereal and milk, the glasses held juice, the mugs held coffee, and the plates held toast for us to enjoy. But as the family left the table, the dishes suddenly became dirty, unacceptable, something to be avoided or done to get the out of the way.

Strange, I thought. What a sudden transformation from clean and acceptable to eat from, and then the minute one laid down the spoon, knife, fork, and left the table, the dish became dirty—something to hide. Hiding and shame raise anxiety and fear. What a puzzling power these dishes have: to produce pleasure; hold the food we enjoy; and then quite suddenly, to produce fear, anxiety, shame, and a need to be hidden.

As I sat there allowing the thoughts to find their own place in my consciousness, another clarity began to surface—not from myself, but from beyond me, another "voice." We pray each day for God to give us this day our daily bread. And dirty dishes? They are sign and symbol that God, once again, this day, has answered that prayer: "Give us this day our daily bread."

The dishes—smeared with the remnants of milk, globs of breakfast cereal, crumbs from toast, and smears of peanut butter—now became icons of God's care and provision. I decided to leave the dishes piled on the kitchen counter so they could speak their kind message for a while longer.

The dishes hadn't changed; I had changed. God had come close and reminded me of the prayer we prayed each day, "Give us this day our daily bread." And with the Spirit's help, my view of dirty dishes was transformed. Rather than being a problem to be avoided and hidden, now they were messengers of God's care and provision. Anxiety and avoidance were transformed into thanksgiving and peace. That is the way of simplicity. Living into simplicity is accompanied by this new and transformed way of seeing. I penned a few lines and stood the card on the windowsill in back of the sink:

Dirty dishes
are sign and symbol
that God
has once again answered
our prayer:
"Give us this day
our daily bread."

I was being led across the threshold from living in the old stories of my childhood into living in the Great Story. A kind of moving house is happening here. In his book, *Lifesigns,* Henri Nouwen draws our attention to this kind of movement: from out of the house of fear into the house of love. He also points out that this house of love "is not simply a place in . . . heaven beyond this world. Jesus offers us this house right in the midst of our anxious world."[3] Here, we live into simplicity.

This is why we see Jesus not being caught up in the anxiety and hostility of Martha when she demands him to order Mary, her sister, to help her. This is why Jesus does not find himself needing to yield to his followers when they hunt him down as he prays in the early morning hours on the mountain and demand, "Don't you know everyone is looking for you?" Jesus has been listening in the presence of Abba, the Architect and Mapmaker for the spread of the good news, and he knew that rather than return to Capernaum, he was to move on—to bring good news to others in other towns and villages. He listens for God's voice and hears the guidance.

Questions for Personal Reflection and Group Discussion

1. Pause and reflect on your own childhood stories.

2. How did you learn to "see" . . .

   - dirty dishes?
   - new persons who moved onto the street?
   - people who were elderly?
   - elderly persons who were severely ill and not able to respond or do much?
   - persons who began attending church, but who had special needs?
   - persons who were different from yourself or your community?
   - what others thought and required you to do, rather than what you knew God was asking you to do?

SEEING AS JESUS SEES OTHERS IN THE WORLD

While having dinner with Simon, a Pharisee (who held the belief that physical and religious purity/ cleanliness made a person righteous and therefore acceptable before God), Jesus receives a visitor who walks into the open courtyard and dining space where he, Simon, and his guests are eating. A woman in the city, who was a sinner, having learned that Jesus is eating in the Pharisee's house, brings an alabaster jar of ointment. She stands behind Jesus' feet, weeping, and begins to bathe his feet with her tears and to dry them with her hair. Then she continues kissing his feet and anointing them with the ointment.

Now when the Pharisee who had invited Jesus sees it, he says to himself, "If this man were a prophet, he would have known who and what kind of woman this is who is touching him—that she is a sinner." (Religious purity included not touching another person who is unclean.)

Jesus speaks up and says to him, "Simon, I have something to say to you."

"Teacher," Simon replies, "speak."

Then turning toward the woman, Jesus says to Simon, "Do you see this woman? I entered your house; you gave me no water for my feet (Washing the feet of one's guests was considered a basic and sacred hospitality, growing out of the Genesis narrative in which Abraham washes the feet of the three strangers whom he invites to stop in the heat of the day, and rest and receive refreshment. These strangers turn out to be the three members of the Trinity who assure Abraham and Sarah that she will give birth to a son in a year's time [Genesis 18:1-15]. Simon had not asked his servants to give Jesus this kind of welcome.), but she has bathed my feet with her tears and dried them with her hair.

"You gave me no kiss (also a form of Hebrew greeting and welcome), but from the time I came in she has not stopped kissing my feet. You did not anoint my head with oil (another Hebrew practice), but she has anointed my feet with ointment. Therefore, I tell you, her sins, which were many, have been forgiven; hence she has shown me great love. But the one to whom little is forgiven, loves little."

Then Jesus says to the woman, "Your sins are forgiven. Your faith has saved you; go in peace." (This story can be found in Luke 7:36-50.)

The question Jesus asks is, "Do you see this woman?" Simon sees this woman through the lens of his belief system and religious practices, which had everything to do with becoming clean—ritually clean. Being ritually clean meant performing many practices which would ensure cleanliness and acceptance before God: the ritual of washing hands, pots and pans, clothes . . . and the ritual of not touching others who were not clean. This would render one unclean. Hence, Simon's distancing, labeling, and judging Jesus to be less than a prophet, otherwise he would have known who this woman was and would not have allowed her to touch him.

But Jesus does know what Simon is thinking, and after telling Simon a short story about forgiveness, he turns toward the woman who is anointing his feet and asks Simon, "Do you see this woman? Do you really see her?"

Jesus invites us to see from another perspective—as he sees. In this narrative, we are offered a window into the kind of mix which dwells within us—a mix which shapes how we see the other. Jesus knows we get caught sitting in the blind corners of religious and cultural traditions, arranging and labeling people accordingly. In this narrative, we are not given the woman's name, only her label: a woman who was a sinner.

Thus, Jesus invites us to sit with him, to be with him, and to learn to see as he sees. Moving to a different place of seeing means leaving the vantage point offered by the rules of society, of the culture. Sitting beside Jesus brings us to the place where we discover that the mix within us is becoming unmixed. And we learn to see others clearly.

I was on a flight home to Dallas and had a layover in Philadelphia. It was noon, so I picked up a salad and a decaf coffee and searched for an open table among the crowd of passengers also eating lunch in the airport. Finally, I found a table pushed up against another, where a middle-aged man sat eating a double hamburger with a soda. It had been a full week of teaching, consultation, and team meetings, and I was tired. An introvert, I did not feel like conversation. All I wanted was a quiet table and some solitude. A couple of minutes after I sat down, this gentleman's cell phone rang and, as he answered, I heard him saying, "What? He hit on you? I told 'im that if he would be good and not hit on 'is mom for two weeks, I would bring 'im a treat. And here 'e is, actin' out. Tell 'im Grandpa'll give 'im a wippin' when I get home!" The call ended.

"That was my daughter," he said. His voice was gruff. "My grandson didn't listen to 'is Grandpa," he continued. "He's not supposed to be hitt'n on his mother."

Quite suddenly, I became aware that I did need to be present to see this man as my neighbor—not just some traveler to avoid because I was tired.

"How old is your grandson?" I asked.

"Three-and-a-half. Just a little tyke."

"Hmm. That's tough. Three-year-olds don't understand time like we do. And they can act out too."

"Yeah, but he's not supposed to hit 'is mom. The social worker is already involved. Told us she might need to take 'im out of the house if we couldn't sort this hitt'n out. Hitt'n makes for trouble," he explained. I was getting the picture: a grandpa who would hit the child in punishment, a single mom, and a little boy who was acting out sometimes. And then a social worker. A difficult and anxious mix . . . and a deep desire.

"It's hard," I said. "You want so much for him to stay with his mom and you."

"I do." He sat back and looked directly at me, then back down at the table.

"My dad beat on me when I was a kid. I mean beat—belts, sticks, you name it. He had a temper. Took it out on me. I didn't tell no one. Not even at school. In school, I was the perfect student. Grades. Behavior. But then one time during football practice, the coach made a bad call, and I don't know what happened. But I exploded. I lit into 'im, shoved 'im to the ground, and then attacked the assistant coach who was pullin' me off the other coach. I punched 'im in the face and then started runnin'. Fast. Someone called the police. The field was cleared. I kept runnin'. Like a machine. No one could catch me. No one. And then I saw her, Miss H., our English teacher, walkin' onto the field—across to the police. 'You don't need to stay,' I heard 'er say. 'I'll stay. And I'll be here for the boy. I'll wait until he stops. And then we'll have a conversation. He's a good student.' The police gradually left. I was still runnin'. Runnin'. She sat on the bleachers. Quiet. Still. Until I could run no more, and I walked kind of slow over to where she sat. 'Here, have a seat P,' she said, quiet-like. We sat side by side for a while, and then she asked me what happened. For some reason, I felt I could talk. That was the first time I told anybody about my dad, the beatin's, and that I didn't know why I had suddenly let go and lay into the coaches." He looked at me again, his gray eyes tired.

I was awed; he had let down and offered me this piece of his life to see and hold.

"So, there was awful violence in your home. Beatings with belts and sticks. And you tried to keep it together at school. Model student. Until something broke and you let go, got violent. Someone called the police. There they were, on the field, and there you were, running like a machine until your English teacher came and sat and waited for you." I kept my voice quiet, spoke gently: "And now your grandson sometimes lets go and hits his mom. And the social worker comes on the field. And you're frightened they'll take him out of the home. You love him a lot." He leaned his head into his hands and stared down at the empty hamburger box and finally nodded.

"There's a cycle," I said carefully. "Your dad beat on you. You sometimes threaten your grandson with a beating. Your grandson sometimes hits his mom."

"Yeah. And I used to spank my daughter when she was little," he confessed.

"How about if you find a family counselor, someone you can all meet with, talk to, like you talked to Miss H.? Someone who can listen to your grandson, you, and your daughter, so the cycle is broken and beatings are no longer part of the mix in how you live together? And in time, you won't need a social worker on the field."

He looked over at me, his gray eyes steadier and more open, and then said quietly, "Thank you. I like that. Maybe we can."

AWARENESS: LEARNING TO SEE AS JESUS SEES[4]

Preparation

Be still. Allow your body to be at rest.

Release any tension. Your body is a good friend; appreciate this gift of God.

Open your attention to God prayerfully, and invite the Holy Spirit to help you see your life as God does.

Reflection

Look back over the last day or week. Let the events unfold and pass before you. What emerges? What persons or events stand out for you? For what are you most thankful? least thankful? Whose story did you listen to? In what way were you aware of the presence of God in their life, their story?

How are you seeing the other? the stranger?

In what way are you aware of them becoming your neighbor—someone to be seen, heard, known?

What attitudes do you notice within yourself?

- *anxiety, anger, sadness, fear, guilt, hostility, grief*
- *faith (your response to God)*
- *hope (your response in the face of difficulties)*
- *love (your response to yourself and to others)*
- *joy (what energizes you and brings you joy, satisfaction)*

Where are your attitudes taking you—toward God, yourself, and others? away from God, yourself, and others?

Prayer
    Be in the presence of Jesus now. Bring your own needs, your confessions, your petitions, and intercession for others. Know that you are heard and loved, forgiven and restored. Simply rest in the presence of God.

CHAPTER 4
Bringing It All Together: Integration

Abide in me as I abide in you . . . I am
the vine, you are the branches.
Those who abide in
me and I in them bear much fruit, because
apart from me you can do nothing.
(John 15:4, 5)

Lord Jesus Christ,
You see how bent over we are
Burdened and captive to the world's habits
Living in the house of fear.
Unburden us
Lift up our heads to see you
Our hearts to love you
To follow you
To the house of love
To make our home in you,
Even as you
Make your home in us.
Amen.

As I write this fourth chapter of *Simplicity*, it is Holy Week, the final week in Lent. During this last week of his life on earth, Jesus draws his followers close around himself and speaks of his desire for them to be one with him and with each other, just as he is one with Abba and Abba is one with him. Jesus tells them again that this week will not culminate with his being hailed as the Son of David, who will now ascend to the throne of the nation of Israel, thus dethroning the cruel but powerful King Herod, and freeing the nation from the occupation and domination of the Roman Empire. Rather, he will be betrayed into human hands, handed over to the chief priests and the scribes, and they will condemn him to death. Then they will hand him over to the Gentiles; they will mock him and spit upon him and flog him and kill him; and after three days, he will rise again (Mark 9:31; 10:32-34). In the midst of their reactions of silence, disbelief, and questions about this dark narrative (Mark 9:32), these disciples continue to argue and fight among themselves as to who will be the greatest when Jesus claims his political and royal place of being the Messiah, the King of Israel. (See Mark 9:33-37.)

Jesus is patient, kind, and incisive. He prays for them, reminds them that his intent is for them to be one with each other, one with him, and one with his Father, Abba—to come home to God and to each other. He also reveals to them the larger battle that evil is waging against them, designed to tear them apart from each other—even from themselves—then from Jesus and God's purposes. (See John 17:14-16; Luke 22:31-34.) He assures them that in the presence of this battle, he has prayed for them, that their faith will be strengthened and that later, after his resurrection, they are to strengthen each other. In community, we do just that: in our presence and care for each other, we become stronger.

We have been on a journey together, and now our path turns toward integration, bringing it all together: living within simplicity. To be honest, we are unable to do this work of integration with our rational mind. We do not have conscious control of the depth of our soul and spirit. Integration is a movement, a transformative happening that comes as a gift: a gift that is the work within us, the work of God making our home within us and doing the "extreme makeover." That used to be the title of a weekly television show that would take us into the house of a family, a family with some kind of special need: maybe a child who was wheelchair-bound, a parent with special needs, or a couple who had adopted several children and now needed more space for their family. The directors of the work would arrange for the family to leave on at least a week's vacation in Disneyland, while a dedicated team of workers descended on the house and worked day and night to transform the house itself and the yard into the kind of dwelling that would offer what the parents and children needed, and where they could, hopefully, thrive within. Only then would the team of workers leave.

Our Holy Friends—God the Creator, Jesus our Savior, and the Holy Spirit—come and dwell within us and are the dedicated team of workers who engage in this work of extreme makeover. However, we are not sent to Disneyland for a week. Rather, we are drawn in to the discovery of God's presence and gradual work over time and more time. And our Holy Friends do not up and leave once a phase of this transformation is done. This is because the transformation is not designed only around things or decor. While we appreciate beauty, color, and design—all of which we discover and give us wonder and joy in creation—if those things become primary, we lose sight of relationship. In his work, *The Active Life: A Spirituality of Work, Creativity, and Caring,* Parker J. Palmer points out that much of our action is really *reaction*. Rather than flowing from "free and independent hearts," such doing depends on "external provocation. It does not come from our sense of who we are and what we want to do, but from our anxious reading of how others define us and of what the world demands. . . . we become cogs in a machine whose every move is forced by what is happening elsewhere in the interlocked system."[1]

The early followers of Jesus were also reacting. They were controlled by a system which demands victory, supremacy, and taking control. Thus, they were not humanly prepared to experience profound loss. That was not on their radar. And as a rule, not on our radar either. But this week, this Holy Week as we enter the Gospel narrative, we find ourselves walking toward Jerusalem, following Jesus towards rejection—being arrested, tried, and then crucified.

What does this have to do with simplicity? Or, with integration; bringing everything together? The transformative work that our Holy Friends are about is designed to free us from being automatons, caught in a web of the lie which insists we are never enough unless we produce more, make more, accumulate more . . . and then some. The transformation is about freeing us to come home to ourselves, who we truly are. And freeing us to come home to God who comes, in Jesus, to bring us back home. The pathway leads through rejection, death, confronting the powers of death and hell[2], and then resurrection.

As I write this fourth chapter, I invite you to enter the Gospel narrative with me, and for us—together—to notice that we will be offered windows into seeing simplicity in motion. We will see congruence between the inner seeing and inner knowing and the outward response. And sometimes we will become confronted with the battle against that movement toward unity and simplicity.

In previous chapters, we have found ourselves being invited into several different homes. We began with our own homes in chapter one and paid attention to clutter—the "in" term that is now given to our having too much of everything, especially in the kitchen, garage, the front closet, and basement. A kind of awakening happens—an awakening to the need to do something about the overload. We also visited Rita and Ralph's home and discovered that because of the crisis of needing to find work, Rita's illness, and the need of a new transmission, their life was far from simple. But as we stayed and listened, we found that kind members of the church also listened, came alongside, and offered help in such a way that Ralph could now drive and find a job.

In chapter two, we began to look more closely at letting go, pruning—various times and seasons in which God comes, texts us, awakens our attention to how we view things, how we sort and discern what to keep and what to let go of, and what stories are steering our personal ship. We visited the home of Mary and Martha, and were present as Martha became kidnapped and thus distracted by her own inner voices as she prepared food in the kitchen, while Mary sat and listened to Jesus.

In chapter three, we dropped in for a short visit in Matt's apartment, as his four-year-old niece asked him if following the stock market on his computer was all that he ever did. We noticed how this question from a little child found its way into his inner soul, and how he became aware of the imbalance of mix within his life. We also visited the home of Janice, my childhood home, and then later, in our family home in Kokomo, Indiana, and paid attention to how we see the ordinary—especially those things we see as dirty and unacceptable, and therefore to be hidden from others. And how God comes and helps us see through and beyond the ordinary. This transforms our perceptions so we can also see as Jesus sees the woman who was a sinner as she comes to see Jesus while he is at dinner with Simon the Pharisee. We became aware of the mix within us, which colors and shapes our perception and response to others, and how it could rob us of simplicity as we learn to walk the way of Jesus.

In this chapter, we will be pulled into a deeper place as we continue to walk the path alongside the followers of Jesus

- who struggle with disbelief and desire for power and victory;
- Mary, who offers a deep gift of presence to Jesus which draws rejection and criticism by others;
- who finally ask the question they have carried but never spoken;
- who boast faithfulness, but betray and run;
- who, at last, after Jesus leaves, are able wait for the Holy Spirit;
- who are sent by Jesus to come and make home within and among them;
- who now open their homes in kindness and generosity, intentional house churches, where Jesus says, "Where two or three are gathered together, I am in your midst."

SIX DAYS BEFORE THE PASSOVER: IN THE HOME OF MARY
AND MARTHA

In the midst of the mounting storm of opposition,
Jesus and his followers seek lodging in Bethany,
almost two miles from Jerusalem. "Judas is brooding in
his mind about crossing the line and defecting to the
opposition. The high priest, chief priests, scribes, and
Pharisees are moving into collusion with Sadducees
and Herodians in a scheme to arrest Jesus with intent
to kill. But here in Bethany a family of friends offers
a quiet oasis of rest and hospitality."[3] Here, as we
gather, we become aware that Martha is at rest in her
generous gift of hospitality. She remembers how Jesus
called her home to herself and to his presence in her
house. She has learned to gather who she is and what
she does around Jesus and the way he offers, rather
than being jerked around by the voices of fear and
shame of not being enough. Lazarus is here. "Both
sisters are thankful . . . Lazarus . . . is able to sit with
Jesus at table. . . . Lazarus has known death, and
he knows the journey back. He had heard Jesus call
his name as he waited in the dark shadow of Hades,
and the gates of death could not (hold him captive
nor) prevent his exodus"[4]—an exodus marked by the
welcome of his family who came close and did the
tender work of unbinding his face and body from the
grave cloths. Mary is aware of what lies before Jesus.
If his followers resist and fight, she does not. What
Jesus has revealed about his arrest and being crucified
settles deep within her, that open and welcoming

space where she receives the mysterious and hidden ways of self-giving and suffering that God is now beginning to reveal.[5]

We are welcomed and invited in, and as we sit at the table alongside Lazarus, Mary, and Martha, we listen as John and Matthew sit with us and share their story. (See John 12:1-8 and Matthew 26:6-13.)

Matthew, the Narrator
John, the Narrator
Judas Iscariot
Jesus
Disciples

Prayer before reading:
Dear Lord Jesus, loving God,
Help me to listen.
Free me from being blind to who you are.
Release me from captivity to the world's ways.
Help me to listen, to see. Amen.

John: Six days before the Passover Jesus comes to Bethany, the home of Lazarus, whom he has raised from the dead. There they give a dinner for him. Martha serves. Jesus, his followers, and Lazarus sit at the table with us. Mary, aware of what lies ahead for Jesus, has purchased a pound of pure spikenard, a costly perfume. After the meal, she brings the fragrant spikenard and kneels to anoint Jesus' feet, then wipes them with her hair. The fragrance, which fills the house, lingers in my memory of this mystical and loving act. But Judas Iscariot, the disciple who is about to betray Jesus, demands:

Judas: Why is this perfume not being sold for three hundred denarii—nearly a year's wages for a laborer—and the money given to the poor?

John: Judas says this not because he cares about the poor, but because he is a thief; he keeps the common purse and has a habit of stealing what is put into it.

Matthew: The other disciples are also angry and heap blame on Mary.

Disciples: Why this waste? For this ointment could have been sold for a large sum and the money given to the poor.

Matthew: Jesus, aware of the group-think reaction and attack, now speaks his order into this hostile mix of criticism and attack. And he asks his own question of these men.

Jesus: Leave her alone! She bought this perfume so that she might keep it for the day of my burial. You always have the poor with you, but you do not always have me. Why do you trouble this woman? She has performed a good service for me. By pouring this ointment on my body, she has prepared me for burial. Truly I tell you, wherever this good news is proclaimed in the whole world, what she has done will be told in remembrance of her.

Some Commentary

The followers of Jesus were still not ready to accept Jesus' words about his arrest, suffering, death, and resurrection. They wonder about this talk of anointing him for his burial. Is he going mad? Is Mary as crazy as he is?

But what about giving to the poor? Jesus is not against helping persons in need. He speaks out against the religious leaders who tithe mint and cumin, but overlook the care of others. Earlier that week, Jesus had been walking along with his disciples and a large crowd on his way to the Passover in Jerusalem. Bartimaeus, who was a beggar and blind, discovered that Jesus was in the crowd. He began to shout, calling on Jesus to have mercy. The persons standing in front of him ordered him to be quiet—wanting this blind beggar to be silent, unseen, and unheard. Such can be the world's order. However, Jesus stood still, heard his cries, and gives a new order: he orders those in front to bring the blind man to him. Such is the order of the way of Jesus.

It is in standing still that Jesus gives us a clue as to how to pause, to stop, to notice, and to be fully present—even if we are in motion with a large group of people who are resistant to slowing down and noticing who or what is happening around them. This is the sign of being led by the Spirit of God, rather than being driven by the mood of the crowd. Once Bartimaeus comes to Jesus, Jesus becomes his servant as he asks, "What do you want me to do for you?" His plea is for his sight to be healed. Jesus hears and heals. Now the disciples are called to welcome Bartimaeus as he joins them on their way to Jerusalem. (See Mark 10:46-52.)

Hence, the disciples know how vital is this giving to those who are in need, and remonstrate out of that. But they are missing something deeper. They have been avoiding Jesus' talk about rejection and death for weeks, and so miss the intent of Mary's gift of presence. They are unable to pause, to stop, and to hear—receive—the message Mary is speaking in her action of anointing Jesus' feet. Mary is responding out of a knowing within her soul and can embrace what is about to happen to Jesus. This congruence, this unity, of how Mary sees and knows and how she responds as she anoints Jesus offers us a window into simplicity. Here, we see harmony between inner knowing and outward action. Here, we see an un-mixedness in her soul and being, even as the disciples are tussling with a troubling mix within and among themselves as they seek to follow Jesus and at the same time reject where he is going.

Questions for Personal Reflection and Group Discussion

1. As you walk into the house within this narrative, notice where you are in relation to the persons gathered there and in their relation to Jesus.

2. What is your response as you see Mary anointing Jesus?

3. How do you react as you hear the criticism of Judas and the disciples?

4. What do you notice as you hear Jesus' defense of Mary's gift and anointing?

5. In what way would you like to express your soul and feelings to Jesus as the days draw close to his arrest, trial, suffering, crucifixion, and burial?

AFTER THE PASSOVER—LATER IN THE EVENING IN THE
UPPER ROOM

We have made the walk back to Jerusalem and are
now in another house whose owner has opened the
space to Jesus and his followers from time to time.
In a room upstairs, we find ourselves in an intimate
gathering after Judas has left to go to the high priests
to betray where Jesus is this night. Jesus speaks some
last words to the eleven. Words spoken just before a
person dies have a clarity all their own. Stripped of
all other matters of concern or consequence in the
life they have lived, now only what is vital is seen and
spoken. Jesus now speaks a new commandment,

> *. . . that you love one another. Just as I
> have loved you, you also should love one
> another. By this everyone will know that
> you are my disciples, if you have love for
> one another. (John 13:34-35)*

These disciples listen as Jesus says this, but do not
linger to truly hear what he is saying. That realization
will come later.

Personal Matters: Questions, Personal and Spiritual Guidance

When Jesus shares that he is going to be with them
"only a little longer" (John 13:33), Simon Peter has a
question: "Lord, where are you going?" (John 13:36).

When Jesus replies that where he is going Peter
and the other followers will not be able to follow him,
Peter declares, "Lord, why can I not follow you now? I
will lay down my life for you" (John 13:37).

But Jesus knows Simon Peter. He sees and knows who this courageous and eager disciple is: a leader, but at the same time a man who hides how fearful he is at the core. Jesus knows the storm coming against himself will also hit this man, and Simon Peter will fold and betray him. And so, Jesus answers him, "I tell you, before the cock crows, you will have denied me three times" (John 13:38).

There are dark forces at work here—back behind the huge move from the songs and shouts of welcome and worship by the multitude as Jesus rode on a donkey into the Jerusalem temple a few days before. It is night; Jesus is about to leave for the garden of Gethsemane where he will pray, but also where Judas would lead the temple soldiers to arrest him. Jesus is about to hand himself over to the opposition by choice as the way through rejection, crucifixion, and through death to new life—and as the way to defeat the dark powers that stand in opposition to God, the power in the voice in the garden of Eden that asked, "Did God say . . . ?" and "God knows that . . . your eyes will be opened, and you will be like God, knowing good and evil" (Genesis 3:1, 5). But Jesus prays . . . and still prays. His name is above every name. And he is victor over the powers of darkness.

Thomas and Philip also have questions they want to ask. Thomas wants to know the way—wants directions to the houses, the dwelling places Jesus says he is leaving to prepare for them. In this intimate inquiry, Jesus leads us into how concrete heaven is.

This is no cluster of ephemeral rocking chairs perched on a cloud somewhere, but a place where there are many, many houses to live in, and we each have a place. We all belong. Where Jesus is going, we will also be going, and he is getting a place ready for us. And he will come back to take us there.

At this, Thomas wants travel directions. He wants a GPS version. And so he asks, "How can we know the way?" (John 14:5).

And Jesus' answer is probably difficult to understand at first: "I am the way, and the truth, and the life. No one comes to the Father except through me. If you know me, you will know my Father also. From now on you do know him and have seen him" (John 14:6-7).

Jesus is shifting the GPS request into a larger, heaven-and-earth-encompassing realm, but with the intent of showing the way back home—the way we lost this side of Eden and have been looking for ever since . . . the way home to God: the God whom we began to fear, to dread coming close; the God whom we saw as the enemy, the one who would see us for what we are—as those who are guilty, ashamed, and naked in this God's presence . . . and from whom we learned to hide our being unacceptable. But now Jesus is saying that he is the way to the Father and that his followers know the Father and have seen him. Seen him? Where? How?

Hence, Philip's question as he now joins in on the conversation: "Lord, show us the Father, and we will be satisfied" (John 14:8).

Years ago, when our youngest son was seven, he asked me a question. It was bedtime, and the evening—late in November's shorter days and longer nights—was dark. I was drawing the curtains in his bedroom, and he said, "Is God like my daddy?"

I turned, went over to his bed, sat down, and thought for a few minutes. Seven years old. How is he thinking? Concrete, tangible thinking would be where he is coming from. And so I replied, "Yes, in some ways, God is like your daddy. God created you, and your daddy also helped make you as a baby. God makes sure you are provided for, and so does your daddy. That's one reason he goes to work at the church each day. And God loves you. And your daddy loves you too. Very much."

"Well, God isn't really like my daddy," he said in reply. Without too much thought, I trod the path I had just laid out and repeated what I said. And this blond-haired, blue-eyed son looked me straight in the eye and repeated what he had just said. I realized at that moment that he already knew what he wanted to say. And he did: "God is a spirit. And you can't hug a spirit," he declared.

I sat a bit longer and then realized what time of the year it was—Advent. And so, I replied, "Yes, God is a spirit. And like the wind, we can't see it when it blows, and we can't hug it either. And to be honest, that's bothered lots and lots of people. We've all wanted to know what God looks like. And we've all wondered about what it would be like to be hugged by God and not pushed away. Your dad never pushes you away. And that's why Jesus came at Christmas. He came as a baby people could hug. And when he grew up, he came to show us what God is like. He loved children and never pushed them away. Instead, he picked them up and hugged them and blessed them. He made God huggable."

It was later, in a conversation with a family therapist, when we got to talking about children and their questions about God. She asked me if my son was visual. I said that he was, very visual. She recommended that I find a picture of Jesus to put up in his room—which I did: a colored print of Jesus in action with his disciples as they stood and sat together in conversation around their boat. And this boy was satisfied. He needed an image in his mind.

And so did the disciples. Jesus answers Philip. And with Philip, all of the eleven and all of us: "Have I been with you all this time, Philip, and you still do not know me? Whoever has seen me has seen the Father. . . . I am in the Father and the Father is in me" (John 14:9, 11).

As we follow Jesus around in the Gospels, we learn what God is like through Jesus' example. This Jesus who welcomes all who come; who does not come as judge to condemn but to find and welcome the lost, the frightened, the poor, the lonely, the sick, the unwanted, the untouchable, and all who turn to him to listen to his voice rather than the multiplicity of voices of the world's system that screams its demands, dangles its promises, and which remind us every day that without what the world has to offer, we will never be in and we will never be enough.

Now Jesus is saying, "You are in. You are coming home. God has a place for you that I am preparing. You are not an orphan. Your name is written. Your birth record shows you are a citizen in God's realm, a member of the heavenly family. We are all immigrants from the world's system and are now accepted without having to have a green card."

Jesus is the way in. This lays at the heart of simplicity. We belong. We are enough, now and forever.

HOUSE MEETINGS: HOUSE CHURCHES AND INTENTIONAL COMMUNITIES

Later, after the Resurrection and after these followers (and some one hundred more) have waited just as Jesus instructed them for the Holy Spirit to come and be within and among them, we find they are now endowed with courage. The Spirit of Jesus is the equalizer within and among them as they meet in each other's homes, pray together, are fully present to one another and serving one another out of their gifts—the spiritual gifts of teaching, faith, pastoral care, wisdom, discernment, healing, and speaking in other languages . . . also, the gifts of tangible help as persons sell their possessions in order to provide for those who are in need, especially widows and those who come from cultures speaking languages other than Hebrew or Aramaic. They eat meals together with glad and generous hearts, and break bread together—remembering the words of Jesus at the Last Supper, to "do this in remembrance of me—remembering my death until I come."

These acts of prayer, presence, sharing gifts, and serving each other become the face, soul, and message of witness:[6] "There was not a needy person among them" (Acts 4:34). Others in the neighborhoods of the city take note, welcome what they see happening, and find themselves among those who feel the tug of God to join in on this new thing, to enter into the blessing so evident before them, and to walk the way of Jesus.

Our presence, our acts, our attitudes, our kindness, our patience, and our generosity all speak of love for one another. When we do this out of love for Jesus, this way of being with one another speaks. It is a witness people see, hear, and notice. Here, evangelism happens. Folks are drawn into the mix of love and goodness in being and in action. The true, deep, inner self sees, feels, and knows that here, in being with one another, goodness happens. God is here. We are drawn home.

It is here—in Mary and Martha's house, in Jerusalem in the house with the upper room, and even in Simon Peter's house in Capernaum which served as a home for Jesus as he settled in that city early in his ministry[7]—that we are being introduced to intentional community: where persons live and meet with one another with the intention of gathering their lives around Jesus, around God. Today, while the institutional church is gradually losing ground in numbers, budget, attendance, and influence, there is a growing and emerging interest in something simpler, something deeper, something that looks more like Jesus.

While flying back to Virginia, in the passenger seat beside me sat a woman who opened a conversation as we traveled. In time, after I had learned she worked as a real estate agent, she wanted to know what I did.

"It may sound strange, but I teach people to pray," I replied.

"I pray," she replied. "But I'm not into church. I stopped going a while ago. Too much talk about money, attendance numbers, and keeping the building up. As if this is what it's all about. I do work one evening a week in a shelter for the homeless, serving dinner. And then another night listening to women who work several jobs but don't earn enough to pay the bills . . . often single parents. I seek to find them affordable housing and help them access other ways the city offers assistance. But I'm not a very good Christian because I don't attend church."

As I listened, I was so aware. There are thousands of persons who feel and say and respond the same way. They are spiritual, concerned, and active in doing many works of kindness, but are not church-attenders. Into this mix of persons who are searching another way, a quiet but emerging movement of the Spirit of Jesus is at work drawing persons toward seeking a smaller community that meets together with intention:

the house church. The Book of Acts offers us windows, along with the New Testament letters, into the life and practices of these scores of house churches—the outward expression of the new thing that God was doing in and through Jesus and the Holy Spirit. This is the way of simplicity. And today, this is a way that God is alive and active in the world.

Questions for Personal Reflection and Group Discussion

1. In what ways have you learned simplicity as you and your group (if you met with a group) have walked the paths offered in this study?

2. Are you aware of tension between various racial or cultural groups in your neighborhood or congregation? How do you respond?

3. How do you find yourself responding to the way in which evangelism happened through the way the early believers lived, ate, prayed, learned, and cared for one another—lived out the way of Jesus' love; cared for the needy among and beyond them?

4. What needs are being met in the local neighborhood through your congregation? What needs could be met?

5. In what way is this ministry a witness—an invitation into knowing the inner and outer needs, hungers, and desires of all are heard and responded to? And thus, how does simplicity then become a reality?

6. How will you continue living into the life of simplicity, the way of Jesus?

NOTES

INTRODUCTION

1. Elaine M. Prevallet, *Reflections on SIMPLICITY,* Pendle Hill Pamphlet 244 (Pendle Hill Publications; 1982, 2015), 2. Elaine Prevallet is a member of the community of the Sisters of Loretto, one of the first Catholic orders of women to be founded in the United States. As part of their life together, the community holds all things in common in a spirit of simplicity, which they discover "requires an uncluttered and unclinging spirit."

CHAPTER 1

1. Born in Japan, Marie Kondo started work as a professional tidier at age nineteen, as friends hired her to tidy up their homes. Based on a deep Japanese acceptance that each thing possesses its own life energy, Kondo invites her audience to sort out their stuff, one room at a time, and to then pick up each piece and be thankful for the well-being or energy that piece has brought. If the item no longer gives a sense of joy or energy, then give it away. Discard it. In this way, we gradually declutter our house of unwanted stuff that de-energizes us. See her book, *The Life-Changing Magic of Tidying Up: The Japanese Art of Decluttering and Organizing* (Ten Speed Press, 2014).

2. Search "The KonMari Method" on a computer for further information regarding her method, also for online guidance.

3. Henri Nouwen, *The Way of the Heart: Connecting with God Through Prayer, Wisdom, and Silence* (Ballantine Books, 1981), 12.

4. A helpful book which offers guidance for listening to our bodies and offering guidance and prayer practices as we turn to listen and tend our bodies is *Prayer and Our Bodies* by Flora Slosson Wuellner (The Upper Room, 1987).

5. Slosson Wuellner, *Prayer and Our Bodies,* 17.

CHAPTER 2

1. Eugene H. Peterson, *Answering God: The Psalms As Tools for Prayer* (HarperSanFrancisco, 1989), 2.

2. When Jesus refers to the Law, he is talking about the Law of Moses contained in the Book of Exodus. This Law gave guidance for the people of Israel to know how to live as God's people, how to relate to each other and to persons in the world beyond their tribes. Also, to know how to relate to money, possessions, and how to become aware that punishment for disobedience was to be measured. Hence, it is startling when Jesus offers a new way forward beyond the Law.

3. M. Eugene Boring, "The Gospel of Matthew: Introduction, Commentary, and Reflections," in *The New Interpreter's Bible, Volume VIII* (Abingdon Press, 1995), 177.

4. We also need an undivided heart in order to love God above all else and all others.

CHAPTER 3

1. Thomas Merton used this term—the false self—to describe the self which emerged this side of Eden.

2. Here, we discover God entering into a marriage covenant with the people: "I will take you for my wife in righteousness and in justice, in steadfast love, and in mercy. I will take you for my wife in faithfulness; and you shall know the Lord" (Hosea 2:19-20). Again, here the "know" is not just head knowledge; it is a fully embodied knowing that permeates the body, mind, soul, spirit, and is expressed in all of life.

3. Henri Nouwen, *Lifesigns: Intimacy, Fecundity, and Ecstasy in Christian Perspective* (Doubleday, 1989), 20, 22.

4. This spiritual practice grows out of a prayer in Psalm 139, a psalm of awareness of God's presence and work across our lives. At the end of the psalm of awareness and gratefulness, we also learn to ask God to help us see and discern any harmful ways we have walked and, in response, to be led by God rather than what is false and not life-giving. This prayerful recollection was formalized by Ignatius Loyola in the Consciousness Examen.

CHAPTER 4

1. Parker J. Palmer, *The Active Life: A Spirituality of Work, Creativity, and Caring* (Jossey-Bass Publishers, 1990), 39. Palmer is a writer, teacher, activist, and a member of the Religious Society of Friends (Quakers).

2. The apostles reveal to us that following his death, Jesus "also descended into the lower parts of the earth. . . . He was put to death in the flesh, but made alive in the spirit, in which he also went and made a proclamation to the spirits in prison" (Ephesians 4:9; 1 Peter 3:18b-19).

3. Wendy J. Miller, *Jesus, Our Spiritual Director: A Pilgrimage Through the Gospels* (Upper Room Books, 2004), 155.

4. Miller, *Jesus, Our Spiritual Director: A Pilgrimage Through the Gospels,* 156.

5. In his letter to the house churches in Colossae, the apostle Paul writes about what had been hidden but now had been made known: " . . . according to God's commission that was given to me for you, to make the word of God fully known, the mystery that has been hidden throughout the ages and generations but has now been revealed to his saints. . . . this mystery, which is Christ in you, the hope of glory" (Colossians 1:25-27). Here, we are given to know that God comes in Jesus to make God's home within us. We learn to come home to God.

6. Within The United Methodist Church, these five practices—prayer, presence, gifts, service, and witness—are the five underlying practices of covenant commitment when becoming a member. See also *Come with Me: Daily Living with a New Monastic Rule of Life* by Wendy J. Miller (Missional Wisdom Foundation, 2015). These five practices become foundational and integrate our being and doing around the way of Jesus with one another and in the world.

7. See Mark 1:29-34; 2:1-12. It is in Simon Peter's house that we see and hear Jesus in deep conversation with his disciples and with many others, who both gather at the door and even break through the roof to get close enough to be healed.